Campus Gho

Haunted Valley... T

MW01074378

By M. L. Swayne

The Pennsylvania State University (Penn State)

University Park, Pennsylvania

Cover Photos: Wikimedia Commons

Table of Contents

Happy Valley or Haunted Valley?

Every College Has A Legend... An Introduction to the haunted history of Penn State

Photo by George Chriss/Wikimedia Commons

Penn State's University Park Campus features the grave of former University President George Atherton. The grave is located next to Schwab Auditorium, along Pollock Road.

Long before students tromped their way to class at Penn State and, in fact, even before pioneers and settlers, drawn by the stories of plentiful game and rich soil, began to till the land, Native Americans sensed that the area now known as Nittany Valley, popularly referred to as *Happy Valley*, was sacred ground.

It was a Haunted Valley. The tribes believed that there were strange powers at work in the valley, powers that shouldn't necessarily be feared, but respected. The powers that inhabited this valley were, for the most part, protective ones.

In the mid 19th century, when the University's early founders searched the region that became known as Centre County for a suitable spot for a farmer's college, they knew little about the spirit lore that surrounded the fertile area like the towering mountains to the east and west of the valley. They were, after all, rational, down-to-earth people looking for a place that could teach scientific principles to young farmers who would use that knowledge to build prosperous farms, then prosperous communities and, eventually, a prosperous nation. They had little time for tales of ghosts and spirits. Little did they know that as they began to lay the cornerstones of the University, they were laying the foundations of Penn State's haunted reputation.

That haunted history technically started in 1855 when the Commonwealth of Pennsylvania chartered a school at the request of the Pennsylvania State Agricultural Society. The school, called the Farmer's High School of Pennsylvania, was a radical idea. Instead of the typical subjects of mathematics, rhetoric, and Greek and Latin languages, the lessons would be centered on agricultural science.

James Irvin, a prosperous iron master, gave the school 200 acres to begin this experiment. When Congress passed the Morrill-Land Grant in 1862, states were permitted to sell federal land and use that money to support colleges and universities. Pennsylvania used its land-grant funds to support what had now become known as the Agricultural College of Pennsylvania.

The University's first major building was soon underway... and so was its first ghost story. In 1863 workers started to build Old Main, a building that would be the hub of the young college. It would contain classrooms, laboratories, offices, and rooms for approximately 400 students. Helping the workers was a mule named Coaly, who dragged some of the limestone blocks from the quarry to the building site. Some people say that Old Coaly never left.

In 1882, George Atherton took the helm as president of the struggling Pennsylvania State College. A strong proponent of land-grant education, Atherton was considered something of a savior of Penn State by University historians. During his presidency, he pioneered engineering classes at Penn State and started an agricultural experiment center that served as an early research lab for agricultural sciences. As Atherton's reputation grew, so did funds from the state government. Even after his death in 1906, Atherton, whose grave is right next to the incredibly spooky Schwab Auditorium, casts a long shadow over the University. It's not just his reputation that haunts Penn State; students and other witnesses say it's his spirit that haunts the campus.

Penn State entered the 20th Century as a solid, but struggling school. By the first third the 20th century, Penn State had over 5,000 enrollments and was soon the state's largest source of bachelor's degrees—and, arguably, the largest source of University-bound ghosts, too. While the main campus grew, the University itself stretched across the state. Responding to Depression-era economics, the University administration under President Ralph Hetzel introduced the branch campus concept. Potential students were finding it hard to raise enough money to cover room and board costs at a distant university. Students also were staying at home and working to help their families. Hetzel's idea was to develop campuses across Pennsylvania, so that students had access to a Penn State education no matter where they lived. As campuses began to sprout up, Penn State's haunted reputation only got richer. Soon Mount Alto, Altoona, Erie and other branch campuses brought their own ghost tales into the Penn State fold.

Later in the 20th Century, Penn State became a leading research institution. President Milton Eisenhower (U.S. President Dwight D. Eisenhower's brother) and his successor Dr. Eric Walker oversaw this explosion in research and development. Penn State scientists became leaders in areas as diverse as dairy science, children's television, building insulation, and diesel engines. While Penn State research scientists worked hard to dispel superstitious thinking that lingered on campus, they had no luck at quieting the students' explorations into the occult and paranormal. Urban legends and tales of poltergeist outbreaks joined the already lofty volume of ghosts of mules, the wandering spirits of dead University founders, and other tales of haunted buildings on the Penn State campus.

Recognizing its status as one of the nation's premier universities, Penn State became the eleventh member of the prestigious Big Ten Conference—officially integrating into the conference in 1990.

Penn State students have never been shy about reporting paranormal phenomenon. In 2001, a group of students got serious about it. That year Ryan Buell founded the Penn State Paranormal Research Society and pushed for it be officially recognized by the University as a student group. It became one of the few—and possibly the only—student paranormal groups at that time. Its mission is to "scientifically and spiritually" explore the paranormal. The group has investigated several hauntings on the Penn State campus, as well as helped clients around the country who claim they are experiencing paranormal occurrences. Each year, the group holds Univ-Con, a conference that brings some of the brightest minds of paranormal research and investigation to Penn State's University Park campus. Attendees have included members of the Sci-Fi Channel's Ghost Hunters team and paranormal research pioneer, Loyd Auerbach.

In 2007, the group became the subject of a docu-drama named, *Paranormal State*.

Like conversations on whether the Nittany Lions will win a national championship or which local bar has the best beer, ghost stories can be the subject of intense debate on campus. Some students are convinced the stories represent real paranormal phenomenon; others tend to see these tales as simply legends and while folklore is a fun and interesting to talk about, these students discounts these tales as true phenomenon.

In the following pages, you'll have a chance to join this debate as we explore the growing body of ghosts who have enrolled at Penn State over the years. We'll also take a look at some of the spirits who haunt Penn State's branch campuses and delve into haunts near Penn State and its branch campuses.

Sacred Ground, Haunted Ground

The fertile ground of Penn State legends and Native American lore

Photo Wikimedia

Mount Nittany looms over Penn State's campus physically and spiritually.

Happy Valley isn't really a valley; it's more like the confluence of two valleys—the Nittany Valley on the west and Penns Valley on the east. Separating the two valleys is a majestic mountain—Mount Nittany.

At more than 2,000 feet high, the mountain dominates the landscape. Although, to be fair, when students come from the Rocky Mountain area, they are more likely to refer to it as a hill. However, Native American tribes who never ventured to the Rocky Mountains were suitably impressed by the height of Mount Nittany. And, if you ask students who have just completed a hike on Mount Nittany—an official rite of passage—they tend to be satisfied with the landmark's status as a mountain.

The American Indians who lived in the area—mostly from the Delaware and Shawnee tribes—named the mountain *Nit-A-Nee*, which comes from an Algonquin word that means, single mountain. Other sources say the word means "barrier against the elements." The mountain serves as a natural barrier against the strong north winds that cut through the valley in winter—as any student who has stood in the Beaver Stadium stands during a cold November game can attest to. Mount Nittany also formed a defensive barrier against enemy tribes.

Whatever the true meaning, these Nittany Valley natives recognized that the area had a special feeling. It was a protected place, a safe place. When white settlers finally arrived, they also sensed this place was special, a place that they began to refer to as Nittany, a corrupted form of the original Algonquin word.

When Penn State was established in 1855 the word Nittany was already in use. About that same time, the first Happy Valley ghost stories began to circulate. Those early storytellers said Mount Nittany didn't arise from a normal geological process, but was formed in a miracle that almost rivals Penn State's victory over Miami in the 1987 Fiesta Bowl. The tale of how Mount Nittany formed—and there are numerous variations—goes something like this:

Nit-A-Nee was the name of an Indian princess who fell in love with a warrior named Lion's Paw. When Lion's Paw died, the princess carried the warrior to the center of the valley and laid him in a grave. She then built a mound over the grave. It took her days to work on the mound, which she finally completed on the last day of the full moon. At the instant she completed the mound, a terrible storm erupted. Lighting flashed and endless rolls of thunder echoed throughout the valley while all the valley's tribes watched the Indian princess, illuminated in the flashes of lighting stretched out her hands over the burial mound. As they watched, the burial mound began to grow... and grow.

And grow.

When the storm had passed and dawn broke, a huge Mountain stood at the center of the valley where the burial mound once stood. And, they say, the spirit of the Indian warrior was passed on to a mountain lion that appeared on the summit of Mount Nittany.

This wasn't the last time Princess Nit-A-Nee would be heard about in a ghostly area folk tales.

Another story has Princess Nit-A-Nee (who just didn't seem to be lucky in love) falling for a French miner named Malachi Boyer, admittedly a pretty strange named for a French man. Nonetheless, the couple romanced in secret, knowing that a marriage between an Indian princess and an oddly-named French miner would not be permitted. They decided to run away. The escape didn't last long. The chief and seven of Nit-A-Nee's brothers caught the couple in an area just outside of Happy Valley.

As punishment for attempting to steal Nit-A-Nee from her family and tribe, Boyer was taken to a water-filled cavern, now called Penn's Cave. While the brothers guarded the entrances to the cave, Boyer frantically swam throughout the cave looking for an escape passage. Finally, as his strength waned, but not his pride, Boyer vowed he would not allow his captors to see him die. He swam to the center of the cave and drowned.

Penn's Cave is now a popular tourist destination in Centre Hall, just a few miles from the University. Visitors can take guided boat tours through the cave where Monsieur Boyer swam his last stroke.

Guides and visitors say that if you are silent and listen closely, you can still hear the whispers of Malachi Boyer as he calls out "Nit-A-Nee... Nit-A-Nee."

Skeptics aren't so sure.

They claim that the origin of both these tales and a lot more stories of the Nittany Valley and Penns Valley area are works of fiction spun by Henry W. Shoemaker. Shoemaker was, among other things, a writer, publisher, folklorist, diplomat, conservationist, and BS artist. Most of the Nit-A-Nee legends can be traced back to Shoemaker. He wrote books—approximately 100 of them—about Pennsylvania and its flora, fauna, animals, caves, mountains, rivers and, most of all, its myths. As a conservationist, Shoemaker hoped to draw attention to the environment so that Pennsylvania residents would want to preserve it as much as he did. One way to do that, he reasoned, was through the preservation of folktales.

Since he often summered in a home in McElhattan, a small town not far from Penn State, he had a deep affinity for the Centre County area and many of his stories are focused on the region's natural wonders like Mount Nittany and Penn's Cave.

Shoemaker co-founded the Pennsylvania Folklore Society and, while helping to create a division of folklore in the Pennsylvania Historical and Museum Commission, also became Pennsylvania's first state folklorist. When he died, many of his papers ended up at Penn State where they're still poured over by the area's budding folklorists.

His critics say that Shoemaker's desire to preserve the region's myths and legends went too far. They say he didn't preserve the legends; he made them up. The tales about Princess Nit-A-Nee, Lion's Paw, and Malachi Boyer were not passed to him by an aged Indian, as he claimed. They were spun from his own vivid imagination. An act like this was a kind of desecration, according to many academic folklorists and Shoemaker's reputation has been tarnished a bit in folklorist's circles.

It might be that when visitors listen to the whispering waters that lap in the void of Penn's Cave, they're not hearing a princess' doomed lover at all. It might be the ghost of old Henry Shoemaker spinning a few more tales about Nit-A-Nee.

Go to the Light, Old Coaly.

Watts Hall

Photo by George Chriss/Wikimedia Commons

The bones of Old Coaly are now located in the HUB-Robeson Center located just down Pollock Road just north of Haunted Old Main and Atherton's grave.

Penn State—once called the Farmer's High School—has bloomed since the days when it was reserved almost exclusively for the education of agricultural students. It's no longer just a school for farmers. However, barns and silos—and the occasional herd of roaming livestock—serve as a reminder that Penn State continues to be a premier agricultural school and research facility.

There are more than cows, sheep, and goats that graze these lush hills and pastures, however. There's one animal in particular that, despite having been put out to pasture—way, way out to pasture—keeps returning to roam the grounds once more. Penn State is the only campus in the nation that is haunted by a jackass--the ghost of Old Coaly.

Coaly was Penn State's first great transfer acquisition. According to official Penn State records, Coaly came to central Pennsylvania in 1857 with his owner Piersol Lytle. Lytle's son, Andy was among the 200 workmen building Old Main.

Joining three other mules and two horses, Coaly was responsible for lugging cart after cart of stones to the site. The boulders that Coaly would drag to the site were mammoth limestone rocks, which would eventually be shaped into blocks that would make up the beloved building named Old Main. (Actually the old, Old Main… but that's another story.)

Fortunately, for Coaly, there is a huge seam of limestone that runs under most of the Nittany Valley. In fact, Coaly only had to tote the limestone from a quarry that was just a few yards away from Old Main to the place where the refurbished version of the building stands today. It's an area now referred to as Old Main lawn, a grassy area located at the intersection of Pugh Street and College Avenue.

Coaly's trek wasn't long, but the hours were killer. Coaly and workmen toiled for over six years to complete the multi-purpose facility that would one day contain the dorms, classrooms, offices, and even laboratories of the University. It was a huge undertaking. The building was five stories tall, a massive structure for the time and especially for a small community in rural Pennsylvania.

When Piersol and the rest of the workmen were finished, Penn State wanted to retain the best worker for jobs that might pop up around the budding University, so the administration bought Old Coaly for $190. It may not sound like much, but the price was steep for a mule in those days and shows just how high the esteem was for this hard-working staff member. For the next thirty years, Coaly worked on University projects and on neighboring farms. (He wasn't the only one to lend a hand—or a hoof—to local farmers. Originally, all students had to spend some time working on farms as part of the terms of admission to Penn State.)

Students loved their co-worker. Never afraid to take on "other duties as assigned," Old Coaly had the added job of being Penn State's first unofficial mascot. If it wasn't for the University's final acceptance of the cryptozoologically-interesting Nittany Lion as its official mascot, the Penn State Haunted Mules may be taking the field at Beaver Stadium during football season.

Like most mascots, Old Coaly was purported to possess magical powers. School administrators and faculty members were shocked to hear the school mule hee-hawing on top of Old Main's bell tower as they arrived for their morning sessions. Students immediately suspected the crafty old creature teleported himself on to the tower. School officials, being the cynical, skeptical types, instead blamed the students for leading Old Coaly up the tower as a practical joke. Although, maybe Coaly was playing along with the prank, too—he was always considered just one of the gang by the students.

When Coaly finally laid his labors to rest on Jan. 1, 1893, the faculty, staff, and student body were unable to depart with the old faithful mule. His skeleton was preserved and displayed in a series of buildings throughout the campus. He spent some time in a wildlife museum located in the original Old Main and spent some time in the attic of the former Penn State veterinary hospital. He then moved to the Agricultural Administration Building and the Ag Arena. Currently, he's found a stable in the HUB-Robeson Center, a student union building in the middle of campus. Officials say that Coaly was moved to be more publically accessible.

It's easy, though, to feel the presence of Coaly wherever you are on campus. He's had clubs and societies named after him, including the College of Agricultural Sciences' Old Coaly Society. Medlar Field at Lobrano Park, Penn State's new baseball stadium, has an eatery called Coaly's Corner.

His presence may be everywhere, but there are certain places on campus where that presence intensifies. During his extended stay at Watts Hall—a dormitory where he roomed with the remains of Penn State's other animal totem, the Nittany Lion—things got downright spooky, according to witnesses who indicate that Coaly's indomitable spirit was alive and kicking in the dorm halls. Students say they saw the ghost of a donkey at the dorm and heard a constant braying warbling down the dark halls.

Even when Coaly's bones left, a little piece remained. There continues to be reports that Coaly continues to make his hard-working presence known in the dorm. Students have been roused from their study sessions and their slumber (and heaven knows what else) when his mournful "hee-haw" echoes down the halls in the middle of the night. The braying is especially persistent when it comes from the basement, where he once stayed.

Old Coaly isn't just all talk.

Students and dorm visitors say on some nights, perhaps when Coaly isn't feeling so vocal, instead of the typical ghostly braying, they say they hear the plodding of hooves echoing as the never-say-quit spirit of Coaly continues his journey down the dark corridors of the dormitory.

It's not just the sound of Coaly that reverberates around campus. There's at least one report of an Old Coaly apparition. One student reported actually seeing the spirit of Old Coaly standing in a dark hall! Obviously the student was disturbed to see the filmy presence of a mule in the middle of a dormitory hall and went to turn on lights. The instant the lights flashed, Coaly began to fade until, eventually, the mule completely disintegrated in front of the amazed witness.

Of course, since good pranks are as coveted as national football championships on college campuses, many victims of Coaly hauntings suspect practical jokers are behind the phantom donkey call. But, when they investigate, there's no sign of human intervention—no slamming doors, no footsteps, and not even after-the-fact rumors that the events were stage. And, as most know, while pulling a prank is easy; keeping it a secret is an entirely different matter, especially when a few beers at one of State College's watering holes can pry the most resolutely shut mouth.

Could it be that really good practical jokers aren't behind these stories, and maybe, a simpler explanation is that Ole Coaly is just too stubborn to head to the light?

Overdue Spirits

Pattee Library

Photo by Nathaniel C. Sheetz /Wikimedia Commons

Pattee Library is placed at the crown of the Penn State mall. Pattee is known as a perfect setting for late-hour study sessions, a maze of bookshelves called "the stacks," and an unsolved murder that may or may not be behind the library's haunted reputation.

Not all the spirits of Penn State seem as content in the afterworld as Ole Coaly, who lived to a ripe old age for a donkey and now seem to be content a stroll around the dorm halls every once and a while.

Other Penn State spirits have a more serious mission. They are expressing their unhappiness because they were taken from the world of the living too soon.

One of the most disturbing Penn State ghost stories is the tale of the murdered co-ed and a story about a restless spirit that continues to search through the rows of bookshelves in Penn State's main library, Pattee Library. Pattee (pronounced Puh-tee) is named after Penn State's pioneering American Literature professor, Fred Lewis Pattee, and was built in part as a public works project. Construction started in 1937 on the initial section and was finished in 1940. The building underwent several expansions. In 1953, the

"Stacks" section of the library was added to help store the University's collection of approximately 800,000 books.

With hundreds of thousands of volumes packed in a dense collection of floor-to-ceiling metal book racks, Pattee is no place for the claustrophobic or pneumatiphobic (someone who's afraid of spirits). Students have dubbed the library's labyrinth of shelves "the stacks" for a reason. The rows are barely wide enough to compensate for the extra Freshman 15—the sudden weight gain students say they experience in that nerve-wracking first year.

It was in those stacks that, late one November afternoon in 1969, fellow students heard an anguished scream reverberate through the library. Students rushed to find the source. There, in one of the oldest sections of the stacks, the first student on the scene discovered Betsy Aardsma, the victim of a tragic stabbing.

Decades after that scream, it's hard for State College citizens and Penn State students to talk about the brutal attack. Crime, let alone murder, is an aberration in Happy Valley. But, through newspaper stories, police accounts, and information passed from student to student, the account of the Aardsma Murder goes something like this:

While many students deserted the campus during the long Thanksgiving weekend, Aardsma, an English graduate student, stayed behind. Aardsma by all account was pretty, popular, and fun-loving. She had a serious side, too. She had been accepted to a Peace Corps mission to Zaire, but decided to attend Penn State, instead. Her friends also said she was interested in politics, in the on-going Vietnam War, the women's movement, and the civil rights movement.

It was that serious streak, too, that led her to Pattee Library while most students were home, or at least not at the library. She met with a professor and walked to the second level of the stacks to grab a book that she needed for a project.

Several witnesses said they saw a woman on the library's second level talking to a man.

And then, the scream.

A group of students who heard the scream raced to the scene. At first glance, one student thought Betsy had simply had a seizure. It wasn't until a small blood stain appeared on Aardsma's shirt that there was any sign of foul play.

Aardsma was taken for medical attention at Ritenour Health Center-check. But it was too late. She died as a result of her wound, a single knife thrust into her heart.

Police never found the killer. But there were lots of suspects and lots of wild rumors. There were theories that a group of men were involved in the killing. It was even suggested that it was a ritual slaying of some kind of cult or twisted club.

Then there was the serial killer angle. One of America's most infamous serial killers, Ted Bundy, had family in the Philadelphia area. His biological father was rumored to be a professor at nearby Bucknell College. Over the years, Bundy joined the list of suspects.

Others believe that it was the act of several men. Police accounts do say a group of suspicious men were seen in the stacks area where Aardsma body was found. They left mysteriously after telling the other students they were going for "help."

Decades after the murder, a killer was never named or captured. The case is still open.

If that story alone doesn't give book worms chills as they wander in the solitude of the library at night, then reports that the cool draft blowing through the stacks as a reminder that the library is never actually deserted surely does.

These stories appear in regular intervals and are repeated in area newspapers and magazines, as well as student newspaper, *the Daily Collegian.*

Witnesses have reported that they often feel an odd, eerie presence when they're in the stacks. Those who have experienced the phenomena say they feel like they're being watched. These claims don't just come from students, even library workers report the strange phenomena, saying that the presence is most keenly felt in the top section of Pattee.

There are also stories of a sudden breeze cropping up from an inexplicable origin. After all, if a person can barely make it through the stacks, surely wind would be blocked.

Reports of something strange happening in Pattee doesn't stop with cool breezes. There have been more solid encounters. Several witnesses have even heard an anguished cry while studying in the stacks. Still others have seen—or thought they have seen—the ghost of a young woman. In one account, a high school girl visiting the library saw a young lady in the stacks. The lady seemed alive enough, but there was something strange about her. First, the school girl noticed the lady's clothes were oddly out of date. And, the give-away, her feet didn't quite reach the ground.

In this case, as well as several other written accounts and tales passed around campus, the witness claims there is a sad expression on the spirit's face.

Paranormal researchers who have studied this case indicate that some spirits remain on the earthly plane when unfinished business remains. An unsolved murder certainly fits that bill.

Another paranormal theory is that the strange happenings in Pattee Library are a case of residual haunting. Like vibrations that are etched into a record that can be played again and again, intense feelings and emotions can be embedded into reality and then are then played over and over. The heightened emotions of a murder can also create residual hauntings. The scream heard in the stacks could be a type of residual haunting called an audio residual, researchers suggest.

The Pattee haunting has other haunted elements, though. A spirit that interacts and, in some reports, even waves or makes facial expressions, goes beyond residual haunting and enters a level of paranormal activity called an interactive—or active—haunting. An interactive spirit, for some reason, wants to communicate with the living. These are spirits on a mission.

But, skeptics point out that unsolved murders can whip up emotions that are then transferred onto random, but natural events. The cold winds from an air conditioner or an open window and whispers echoing down the hall could account for some of the strange goings-on in Pattee, for example. These things in themselves aren't paranormal at all; but in the right environment (for instance in a huge library that was once the scene of a murder) a breeze or a whisper is given a supernatural meaning by the witness.

Whether it's supernatural or a case of high-strung curiosity, students wandering the stacks still can't help asking themselves:

Is this spirit lingering in the stacks as a constant reminder to solve this mystery?

Is it the echo of a murder victim's chilling scream or a cry of a ghost hoping for justice?

Is this just a college morality tale passed around to reinforce a message to keep aware and to stay safe?

Paranormal Outbreaks

Campus-Wide Supernatural Encounters

Most of the ghost stories follow a pattern at Penn State. There's a haunted area like a building, a grave, or grove of trees; there's a subject who causes the haunting, for instance, a founder, a murder or suicide victim and there's an agent, or someone who witnesses the spirit manifestations.

Not all hauntings fit this pattern. Dubbed an "outbreak" by paranormal experts, this supernatural activity occurs in bursts of strange and highly spooky activity that defy the bounds of the traditional and benign campus ghost tale.

In fact, there have been several of these outbreaks at Penn State and have now become their own campus genre.

The outbreak is not connected to places. These spiritual manifestations occur in relatively-new dorms with no prior history of supernatural activity.

Causes are also hard to pinpoint. While some accounts blame suicide victims or occult-oriented games, the facts of the case rarely bear these out.

The two best reasons for the outbreaks: it's the human mind that's causing these hauntings.

But, even that school of thought is divided. On one side of the argument, skeptics say that there's nothing supernatural about these incidents. Students with overactive imaginations are turning natural events into paranormal encounters.

The other camp believes that overactive imaginations may certainly be the cause of the activity, but that the focused consciousness can actually influence reality. These overactive imaginations aren't just capable of producing fictional ghost stories; they can create disturbances in the real world. The folks who support this position cite well-documented cases of poltergeists and telekinesis (or the mind's ability to influence reality).

Poltergeists reportedly can move objects and cause electromagnetic interference. As we'll see, these strange effects are all mentioned in the stories about Penn State's paranormal outbreaks.

Interestingly, poltergeist encounters usually center around a human agent. The agent of the haunting is typically young and stressed out. Anyone who's ever been on a college campus the week before finals can probably find these exact conditions.

Whether it's real phenomena or just the power of suggestion is for the reader to decide, but we'll start our exploration of paranormal outbreaks at Penn State with the first sample: the Runkle Hall poltergeist.

Room 318... Runkle Hall

Any student of parapsychology will tell you that "poltergeist" is a German word for "noisy, or rumbling, spirit."

It specifically refers to a ghostly manifestation that is more vandal than spirit. Like a drunken frat boy, poltergeists enjoy whooping it up— throwing books, smashing dishes, shutting doors, and instigating a myriad of other, mostly harmless, but annoying (and often extremely scary) pranks. Poltergeists have a long history. In fact, Romans were among the first people to report the rebellious spirits and, if you can out-party the Romans, you're causing quite a stir.

Over the years, and especially since the release of the Steven Spielberg classic movie, "Poltergeist," the list of phenomena associated with this type of haunting began to grow. Mysterious smells, strange lights, apparitions, and the occasional child being sucked into an inter-dimensional television set are all lumped onto the poltergeist's rap sheet. Paranormal investigators caution against blaming poltergeists for these types of hauntings, saying that these extreme cases of paranormal activity are more likely caused by non-human or interactive spirits.

Some parapsychologists say that poltergeist isn't a ghost at all, but a form of telekinesis, or "mind over matter," generated by a frustrated, but very much alive, human. In the majority of poltergeist outbreaks, the activity is centered on a young woman—usually a teenage female. There is also a pattern to poltergeist activity. It usually starts with the movement of random objects. Cups move. Glasses fall. Cupboard doors open by themselves. Then this random and innocent behavior can intensify. Lights flash or explode. Large pieces of furniture—chairs and tables—shake and move.

Whatever a poltergeist is, it can be pretty creepy. If a poltergeist visits a college dorm—well, that's double creepy.

Just ask the occupants and resident administrators in the mid-1990s who encountered what quickly became known as the poltergeist of Runkle Hall. Runkle is a peculiar L-shaped building in a collection of dormitories at the northern edge of campus collectively called North Halls.

No one knows exactly when the poltergeist phenomena began. It's always difficult to pinpoint the exact time that poltergeist activity begins for two reasons. First, the manifestations can be easily attributed to normal human-inspired pranks and naturally-occurring phenomena and, second, the activity starts out small and gradually builds into a crescendo of outrageous and sometimes, violent, displays.

There were rumors of something strange about Runkle Hall for years, but the poltergeist activities hit its terrifying peak in the early- to mid-90s.

In 1992, the events seemed to be centered in one room—room 318—and on one girl. The subject of the haunting wasn't just an average student who may have had a little too much to drink at an end-of-week mixer. According to reports from the Daily Collegian, Penn State's student-run newspaper, she was the floor's resident administrator (RA).

A loud banging kept the RA up one night—a loud banging that seemed to have no explainable source. This sound was different from the noises usually encountered at a dorm. She said it sounded like someone was pounding a hammer, or fists, into the wall with alarming ferocity.

If that didn't make sleep a little difficult, her bed started to heave in and out as if it were breathing. Then the banging got worse. Lights flickered on and off. Objects moved or disappeared altogether.

Resident administrators are trained to be cool in situations like this and this RA searched for natural sources to these problems, something that she overlooked. She wondered if some of her wards were playing a prank on her, perhaps to get even with her for enforcing the dorm rules. It might also just be a mechanical glitch.

She called in the University service specialists who scoured her room for the source of the disturbances she described. No luck. And the activity wasn't just continuing; it seemed to be increasing in ferocity.

Being the sole witness of this activity, the student began to question her own sanity. She decided to bring some friends in as witnesses—and maybe some moral support. The poltergeist wasn't shy around the witnesses and the activity flared up with an unprecedented fury. The girl and he friends fled the room and the poltergeist activity. When they returned to her room, the Runkle poltergeist decided he needed a little privacy. Even though she didn't touch the lock on her hasty exit, she discovered that she was locked out of her room.

Six years later another student was assigned to Room 318. She, too, was driven out.

This student said that she could hear strange mumbling that again seemed to be coming from the walls. It troubled her that she could not make out this strange language.

The reports of this haunting mirror the events of the first Runkle Hall poltergeist encounter. Items moved—or were hurled, more accurately. Lights flickered on and off without any sign of electrical problems, or a human agent.

And then there was the incessant pounding. The student told dorm leaders and fellow students that someone—or something—was pounding the walls violently.

It finally became so bad that she asked to be reassigned to new student housing. The poltergeist, content with the havoc that ensued, didn't seem inclined to follow her and didn't seem to bother the new resident. Sometimes, roommates are just fickle that way.

Other outbreaks occurred. A resident in another Runkle room--Room 313--encountered bizarre behavior. Again, objects were thrown around. Unlike other outbreaks, however, this poltergeist had a decidedly Spanish flavor. The student said that her television was often turned to the Spanish channel, even though she never watched that station. And, even though it's not the best thing to do, paranormally speaking, a group of students decided to communicate with the spirit with an Ouija board. The poltergeist—or ghost, or demon, or whatever—would only answer when the questions were in Spanish.

Creepy? Si.

Campus authorities investigated the incident, but never arrived at a satisfactory explanation.

Those more inclined to the paranormal did come up with a few explanations. Some suggested it was a poltergeist.

However, the Runkle poltergeist doesn't easily fit into the normal, or is it paranormal, definition of a poltergeist. Parapsychologists say that poltergeists seem to attach themselves to a human source and that the activity revolves around this agent. Many times the poltergeist activity centers on a troubled, but socially stilted kid. Like an inner vandal, the poltergeist acts out when the child can't. While most poltergeists appear during that subject's perilous journey between childhood and adulthood, known as puberty, it's not out of the realm of possibility that the rigors and stress of college life could cause a poltergeist to appear.

Poltergeists don't seem to be attached to rooms or buildings the way the Runkle spirit does, either.

Another theory about the Runkle Hall case: the room is haunted by a ghost of a student who committed suicide.

The building was relatively new, built in 1957. That's a short time to be collecting the number of powerful entities said to room at Runkle Hall. And, despite rumors to the contrary, reports indicate that no one ever committed suicide in Runkle Hall, although a student did commit suicide in nearby Leete Hall.

Runkle, still others propose, is haunted by a non-human entity, maybe even a demon. The spirit not only seems to be interactive, but a bit malicious.

Not everyone believes that Runkle is haunted by a poltergeist, a demon, a non-human entity, or even a Spanish television junkie. These skeptics say that new environments, new people, and a little extra stress can cause the imagination to work overtime. In these conditions, people can jump to paranormal conclusions for what is actually simple, natural phenomenon.

Pipes can cause knocking sounds in walls.

Forgetful minds can misplace objects.

Heating and air conditioning vents can cause breezes that may be mistaken as breaths.

Whatever or whoever the source, natural or supernatural, the Runkle Poltergeist hasn't been heard from lately.

Poltergeists, it seems, like good soldiers, never die, they just fade away.

East Halls

While the Runkle Hall poltergeist has seemed quiet, it hasn't ended all dorm-related paranormal activity at Penn State.

In 2007, members of Penn State PRS investigated another haunting, this time at East Halls. A freshman student said paranormal activity started when she began to experiment with an occult game called *100 Candles*. Based on a Japanese occult method, the game is reputed to summon spirits. Players gather before midnight and light a group of candles and tell a ghost story. When the story is finished, a candle is blown out and the next speaker tells a paranormal tale. Once all the candles are blown out, the group will have their own paranormal experience. Unfortunately, critics say this just opens up the psychic pathways and these one-time supernatural occurrences just might not stop.

According to the student, that's what happened to her. The game worked and her room became permanently haunted. She said she saw the spirit of a girl in the bed next to her, even though her roommate was not in the building.

A boyfriend of the student also experienced weird feelings when he was in the room. Other students witnessed dark forms and a palpable presence.

The PRS gang couldn't find any solid evidence or reasons for the haunting.

Keller Building

Another paranormal outbreak occurred in the 1990s at the Keller Building, located at the southwestern edge of campus.

The details are sketchy but the story starts when the building served as a dorm. According to reports, just like the unfortunate residents of Runkle and East Halls, a student was driven from a room by an entity. When the student returned to the room with help, the door was either locked, or an evil presence was holding the door tightly in its grasp.

As they stood at the door, the group of horrified students listened as someone or something inside the room was systematically trashing the room like a frat boy on a bender.

Crashes, bangs and rips echoed from the supposedly empty room.

When they finally managed to open the door, the outbreak instantly stopped, although the room was a complete disaster.

There's no word on if there were any repeat performances by this entity or poltergeist.

Pollack Laptop Library

Students consider Pollack Laptop Library, located in the Pollack Undergraduate Library, to be Library 2.0. The library has everything a student needs to conduct scholarship in the 21st century. They can work on multimedia presentations, design web pages, and print out documents.

While the resources are definitely new school, the paranormal happenings are old school. Stories have filtered out that the library is haunted by an entity and, by all accounts, he (or she... or it) isn't a very happy entity.

Some students have heard a growling noise. Witnesses who have heard the growl describe it as a cross between a dog and a human. Paranormal experts might call it inhuman.

Voices are also heard—often arguing—in the library, too. And these are the types of voices that can't be shushed by the librarians. When people go to investigate the origin of the arguments, there's no one there.

There have even been reports of misty apparitions floating through the east side of the library.

Since the library is new (dedicated in 1999), no one has advanced plausible theories on why the library is haunted. Skeptics say it's just college hijinx; believers say it's just another sign that the University's spirits have successfully made the transition to the 21st century.

"Schwaboo" Takes a Bow

The ghost or ghosts of Schwab Auditorium

It's hard to put an end to rumors of campus spirits. Ghost stories, propelled by the unencumbered spirit and boundless creativity of youth, circulate naturally in universities.

And it doesn't help when you dig a grave in the middle of campus.

And that's exactly what you'll find smack dab in the middle of the Penn State campus.

George W. Atherton, the seventh president of the university from 1882 to 1906, was credited for both saving Penn State from bankruptcy and leaving a surplus of Penn State ghost stories.

Atherton was an educational pioneer who expanded the University's programs beyond its agricultural core to include engineering courses and more liberal arts classes. Atherton also reconnected the college with the community by seeking input from area businesses. Today, Atherton's name is fixed on buildings and streets throughout the University and State College, the community that grew up around Penn State.

Atherton's final resting place is in a simple, marble grave on Pollock Road. It's a fitting memorial for someone who gave so much to create Penn State. But Atherton's legacy is far from dead and buried. Right next to the grave is Schwab Auditorium, reportedly the most haunted buildings on campus.

Coincidence?

Offering the grave's proximity to the theater as evidence, some students and witnesses say it's Atherton who haunts Schwab and is behind the litany of bizarre events. The students even have a name for the spirit or spirits that inhabit Schwab: Schwaboo.

Students continually complain of missing objects at the theater. They place a pen or notebook down and a second later it has vanished. Witnesses have also seen curtains move by themselves and, when the brave decide to investigate, they find no breeze, no draft. It's as if someone invisibly passed by the curtains and created a slight wave of fabric.

Is it just Atherton making his rounds and checking in on his beloved students?

But Atherton is just one of the spectral suspects behind some of the creepy theatrics of Schwab Auditorium, a theater that boasts of dozens of brilliant actors and musicians and reportedly a troupe of ghostly celebrities.

The 972-seat auditorium was built between 1902 and 1903 due largely to a contribution given to the university by Charles M. Schwab, a leader in Pennsylvania's booming steel industry and one of the state's richest men. The tycoon, born in the small nearby community of Williamsburg, Pa., was also a member of Penn State's board of trustees.

At one time Schwab was the right-hand man and hand-picked successor of Andrew Carnegie, Pennsylvania's legendary steel and iron magnate. Indeed, Carnegie donated money for the Carnegie Building, the current home of Penn State's Department of Communication, which sits across the street from Schwab Auditorium. It was Schwab who helped Carnegie sell his steel empire that became U.S. Steel.

But Carnegie and Schwab had a falling out. Carnegie didn't approve of Schwab's new hobby—gambling. Carnegie may have been on to something. Schwab's gambling losses began to take their toll on his fortune. What Schwab couldn't give away or gamble away, was grabbed away by the stock market crash of 1929. Far from the mansions and fast-lane lifestyle, Schwab died in a small apartment in 1939.

Some say Schwab is a more likely suspect for the bizarre goings-on in the theater. There have been coat and shirt-tugging incidents that have been blamed on Schwab. People report that there are noticeable tugs at their clothing. When they turn around, no one is there.

Then there's the famous empty seat trick. Some performers and audience members have watched in horror as a seat lowers all by itself, like someone is sitting down and taking in the production.

Perhaps Schwab stays on campus just to make sure his nemesis, Carnegie, doesn't try to one-up him with a building a new library. He's also just as busy in the afterlife as he was in life. Schwab is the suspected source of a few more ghostly visits, including the haunting at Hotel Bethlehem.

More Paranormal Encounters

Whoever or whatever the source, the theater has been the center of even more paranormal performances.

Hagan King, a Penn State student in the early 1970s, told his story in the Sept./Oct. 1998 edition of *The Penn Stater* magazine. King said he had the surreal luck to be the last soul in Schwab Auditorium on evening in 1970. At least he thought he was the last soul...

King told *The Penn Stater* that he felt like someone was watching him. He looked up at the stage and discovered two figures standing, or perhaps floating is a better term, on the stage. The figures seemed to hover above the stage-right section of the stage and stare at him. One figure appeared to be bigger than the other.

On another occasion, King said he was startled by a noise and saw a shadowy form flutter in and out of a doorway. King also told *The Penn Stater* he was one of many witnesses to feel the infamous tug. He felt a tug on his arm while he was working offstage, when he turned to look, expecting to find someone trying to get his attention, there wasn't anyone next to him, or even close to him.

King wasn't the only one who experienced dramatically weird events in the theater. Another article from *The Penn Stater* retells the story of Tom Hesketh, a technical coordinator and production adviser at Schwab. Hesketh said he was working in the attic of the building—a particularly haunted spot by some accounts and an extremely creepy place by all accounts. He attempted to retrieve a pair of cutters and discovered that they had disappeared, even though he knew he had just laid them down a few seconds before. He checked everywhere—in his tool box and on the catwalk—but couldn't find them. After, reluctantly deciding he had simply lost the tool, he locked up his tool box in a cupboard, and left. The next day, he was surprised to find the cutters laying on top of the box, in plain view.

Atherton and Schwab aren't the only suspected spirits who haunt the theater. According to *The Penn Stater* article, two other workers have come forward about their encounters with ghosts in Schwab Auditorium, but, their descriptions don't easily fit the typical theories that blame Atherton or Schwab for scaring the heck out of Schwab employees and visitors.

While working at the theater, Peter Zimmerman told *The Penn Stater* that he saw a figure standing in the middle of the stage. At first, Zimmerman thought it was a female co-worker. He called out to her, but it wasn't a "her" at all. To Zimmerman's rapidly unbelieving eyes, the shape began—more and more—to take on the appearance of a man with long hair. Zimmerman, his curiosity obviously stoking his courage, drew closer to the figure. After he called out to the man, or woman, or hippie, the figure glided to the right side of the stage, approached the wall, and disappeared right through it!

Zimmerman left the building for a few moments to compose himself after this brush with the mysterious. Who could blame him?

Zimmerman's account sounds eerily similar to a story told by another Schwab worker, the general manager of Penn State's Center for Performing Arts, Dave Will. In this case, Will told *The Penn Stater* he was working in the theater late one night in 1972. A figure—cloaked in gray mist—appeared next to him and slowly took the shape of a man clothed in Revolutionary War-era garb. Just like Zimmerman, Will described a man with long hair. The encounter lasted a mere ten seconds, according to Will.

Will explained the phenomena away, telling himself that the man was a figment of his imagination. But, after a second encounter with the gray man, his confidence began to fade. In 1977, Will saw the figure again—this time in the basement—and became a believer.

Zimmerman and Will's reports raise some interesting questions. If the building was constructed long after the Revolutionary War, does the haunting predate the auditorium, or even the university? Could a ghost have haunted the woods and fields that became Penn State?

Others have a different theory. Perhaps the long-haired trooper is not a soldier at all, but an actor permanently typecast as a soldier.

Could it be?

In the paranormal world, an actor haunting an old theater isn't much of a stretch. After all, it's always hard for actors who are basking in the adulation and applause at Schwab to take that final curtain call.

Here's to You Mrs. Atherton

Old Botany Building

Photo by George Chriss/Wikimedia Commons

Old Botany Building is situated just across the street from the profoundly haunted Schwab Auditorium. Next to the imposing granite and stone structures that dominate the campus of Penn State, Old Botany Building is small and quaint.

Just because it's small, doesn't mean it isn't special to Penn Staters. The cottage-like Old Botany is also the oldest academic building that is still standing on campus, built in 1887. (Hence the "old" part of Old Botany Building.)

It was also designed by F.L. Olds, who used drew on Richardsonian Romanesque as an influence when he came up with plans for Old Botany. The style is based on the work of Henry Hobson Richardson, a Boston architect, whose works include famous places like Boston's Trinity Church and the Allegheny County Prison.

Old Botany has two stories, plus a basement and an attic. The first floor is surrounded by beveled limestone and the second floor is red brick. A greenhouse, which was attached to the west end of the building, was removed in 1940.

Besides being architecturally significant, Old Botany is paranormally significant, according to area ghost busters, students, and staff.

The ghost of Frances Atherton, the wife of George W. Atherton, has reportedly been seen in Old Botany.

And it would be just like France—or Fanny—to keep tabs on the University.

According to information from the State College Women's Club, Frances was every bit the pioneer and innovator that her husband was. Fanny, as most people called her, was a trained teacher and started her career in education when she was 17. She was passionately devoted to improving the lives of women in the State College community and established the State College Women's Literary Club. Members met to read their own papers and listen to guest speakers offer their insights on literary and historical matters.

Fanny's presence is detected all over campus. Atherton Hall is named after her, not her husband. There's even a legend that the University wanted to keep Fanny's dedicated presence around campus so much that they buried her body in the attic of Old Botany.

While that seems to be a legend, at best, the attic is the focus for most ghost stories at Old Botany.

Fanny, they say, can be seen peering out the attic windows looking out at Schwab Theater and onto the grave of her husband. Some say she wears a sorrowful, almost desperate, expression, leading to speculation that she is not happy with the street—Pollock Road—that separates her from her beloved husband. It seems as if this spirit, who can seemingly transcend time and defy death, can not cross the road to visit the tomb of her famous husband.

Maybe Fanny can't walk across Pollock Road, but that doesn't stop her from strolling around campus. As we'll see, Fanny shows up at several other haunted hot spots around campus.

The paranormal phenomenon at Old Botany isn't restricted to apparitions and walking ghosts. Penn State staff reports strange goings-on in Old Botany. One staff member has collected a long list of paranormal activity over the years of service. In one case, the employee placed her key in a door and it magically swung open, even though the chain and bolt, which kept the door securely fastened, was never touched.

It might have seemed like a welcoming gesture, until the employee looked inside. A roll of carpeting that had been thrown away the day before was placed in front of the doorway. The employee wisely locked herself in her office. While she say there (quivering in fear no doubt), she heard the front door open and footsteps echo up the stairs—although no one appeared to be in the building.

Ten terrifying minutes later, a faculty member arrived at work. The employee immediately went to meet her rescuer. They both heard books thudding on the floor. Summoning the nerve to investigate, they found an office door open and the lights on. The office was never used and whoever was responsible for opening the door and turning on the lights was not there... at least that they could see.

Over the years, staff have encountered more than the normal mechanical and electrical glitches in Old Botany. Printers stop working. Fuses blow unexpectedly. Machines break down. Some skeptics might chalk this up to normal office problems. Those skeptics, believers charge, never saw the peculiar staff photo taken a few years ago.

The picture shows the staff smiling in front of the building. One man isn't smiling. He's staring out of the upstairs window in Old Botany.

A man nobody knew and a man no one ever saw again.

A Ghost Walk to Remember

Near Old Botany Building

If mules can haunt Penn State, why not a grove of trees?

Behind Old Botany Building, there used to be a path that stretched between magnificent spruce and pine trees. On the busiest times and in broad daylight, the Ghost Walk, cushioned by this lush wall of trees, was quiet, cool, and serene. Its seclusion made the area perfect place for students to meet and its reputation as a lovers' lane was famous, or maybe infamous.

In the dark of night, though, many former students said they would choose alternate—and better lit—routes to get to their destinations. The small section of campus was just too unsettling at night.

And then there were all of those stories about the little path between buildings...

The grove of trees was planted by William Waring, a professor of horticulture in the 1860s. Little did he know that when he planted the grove, he planted the seeds for a ghostly campus legend.

In one of those stories, Frances Atherton, appears again. She's wearing the same mournful expression, is seen traveling through the area, like she's taking the Ghost Walk. Frances makes it just to Pollock Road, just in sight of her husband's grave, but never crosses. What holds her back is not readily apparent from the tale.

A 1928 edition of the Daily Collegian indicates that the ghost isn't Frances; the apparition is that of a dead student. Legend has it that in the 1860s a ferocious blizzard hit the State College area. Despite warnings, one student tried to trek home during the blizzard, but never made it. The student was walking on the tree-lined path that leads directly to Old Botany and froze to death. The body was discovered near where the Burrowes Building now stands on campus.

There are other more natural explanations for the supernatural reputation of the Ghost Walk area. According to university information, another botany professor made a double exposure photo of his daughters and their friends standing in the Ghost Walk. The resulting photo has an eerie, ghostly quality that skeptics believe triggered the haunted stories.

In any event, in 1929, most of the trees were removed. Only a single Norway spruce and dozens of great stories remain. Many are convinced that people are actually witnessing the reenactment of that fateful winter walk when they see the shadowy figure strolling down the area now called *the Ghost Walk*.

Spooky House Mothers: Gumshoes and Fanny

Atherton Hall

Photo by George Chriss/Wikimedia Commons

Atherton Hall was named after Frances "Fanny" Atherton and is another spot to find Fanny's ghost on campus.

Penn State women have come a long way, baby. Penn State ghosts? They're still pretty much where they've always been.

Before World War II, faced with an increasingly larger female student population, Penn State officials built Atherton Hall, named after Frances "Fanny" Atherton, the better half of Penn State's original power couple (before Joe and Sue Paterno). The building was the first residence hall on campus created just for women.

At that time, the lives of female residents in Atherton Hall—or "Athertonites" as they were called—were strictly monitored. There was a strict curfew time and on date nights, the students were required to say goodnight to their beaus outside the building in an area called the sunken quad.

Who policed the curfew?

The University employed a few secret weapons. According to the student newspaper, Atherton rooms had electronic censors—which would be a pretty modern idea for pre-War Penn State. If anyone tried to leave the dorm, an alarm was sounded.

On the other end of that alarm, was the real secret weapon—the house mother. The house mother, as her name suggested, was looked up to as a friend and mentor... but, don't be fooled, she also watched over the students with an eagle eye. One Atherton Hall house mother ascended to a legendary status normally reserved to prize-winning professors and football coaches. Residents nicknamed her Gumshoes. They called her Gumshoes because as she made her late night rounds on the floors, her shoes made a unique "smacking" sound.

The house mothers have faded into the past, part of a different era and a different Penn State. Not all the house mothers got the news. Residents of the new Atherton Hall say that Gumshoes continues to make her rounds. Her footsteps fill the halls with that distinctive smack. Students say they hear the footfalls late at night, or early in the morning—prime time for curfew violators.

There are other spooky goings-on, according to residents. More than a few students have complained that their doors mysteriously open and close on their own. Is this a sign of poltergeist activity? Or is there a simpler explanation is Gumshoes checking in on them?

She apparently has company in the spirit world.

Other reports that filter out of Atherton Hall say there's one more ghost haunting the halls of the dorm. Unlike Gumshoes who is normally heard but not seen, this ghost isn't afraid to show up. Her apparition has been seen gliding both inside Atherton Hall and on the grounds that surrounds the building.

Most witnesses believe this apparition is the ghost of Fanny Atherton.

No one can guess what she's up to on these spirit walks. Fanny was dead before the building was constructed and there's no evidence that the site had any special meaning to her. And, it's a pretty long walk (or glide to be more descriptive) from her old haunt at Old Botany to Atherton Hall. But, what's bi-location to a reality-defying spirit anyway?

Then again, maybe Gumshoes called off sick and Fanny is filling in as house mother?

Business As Unusual

The Beam Building Haunting

The Beam Building officially opened in 1957—not a very lucky year by some accounts—as a dormitory. Not only was the haunted Runkle Hall built the same haunted year, but there were also a slew of student deaths, the Daily Collegian reports. The Beam Building was also part of that mysterious North Hall region that, inexplicably, is a haunted focal point on campus.

Some students and paranormal investigators believe that the Beam Building, like its sister buildings of North Hall, is haunted by lives cut short, too short. Reports of suicides figure heavily in haunted college lore. For young people in the prime of their lives and health, a story of fellow students committing suicide is a brush with mortality.

Campus legend has it that one of the deaths that year was in the Beam Building, in the second floor men's room to be specific. A despondent male student reportedly hung himself on a pipe that stretched across the ceiling of the bathroom.

This disturbing event caused a stir in the building, students report, but the news of a suicide didn't come close to the buzz to follow. Almost immediately after the death, strange activity was reported in the Beam Building. Rumors were passed that it was haunted. Some classify the activity as mere poltergeist activity: chairs and tables were moved and books would drop off their shelves. Other reports indicate it was an interactive spirit visiting the dorm. Doors that mysteriously locked and unlocked themselves and a host of other incidents made residents and guests wonder if the spirit in Beam was trying to communicate. Was the spirit locking and unlocking doors as a sign that he was trapped? Was he moving tables to get attention... and help?

Those pleas, if they were pleas at all, by the spirit went unnoticed. The building was switched from dorm use to class and office space for the Business Department. Some people indicate the Beam poltergeist, as some students referred to the spirit, influenced the decision to change the building from a student resident hall to an office building for a no-nonsense group of business faculty. If that's the case, it seems to have worked. The number of reports of haunted behavior has diminished, if not disappeared entirely.

There are other explanations. Skeptics point out that all the phenomenon reported in the Beam Building could be explained through natural phenomena. People can forget they unlocked a door, for instance. The report of suicide—true or not—merely adds context to the events. In other words, it places a supernatural tilt to common, natural effects.

The Beam Building was recently changed to the temporary home for Penn State Dickinson School of Law. There are those who say they would much rather have a run-in with a poltergeist than a team of highly-trained lawyers.

An Urban Legend Stalks Brumbaugh Hall

Brumbaugh Hall

In the eighties, before most people even knew what an urban legend was, a scary story began to make its rounds among students on the Penn State campus.

The story had many variations and was probably changed as it was passed from student to student. It went like this:

Jeanne Dixon, a famous astrologer and pop culture prophet, was on the Johnny Carson show... or the Letterman show.... or any late night show. Anyhow, she was on a television show. During that show, she made a stunning prediction: there would be a mass murder of students at Penn State. Well, maybe she didn't exactly say Penn State. She may have said that there would be a mass murder at the tallest woman's dorm in the country—at least, that's what some students heard. But Penn State has the tallest woman's dorm... at least that's what students heard.

The massacre would occur on the grand-daddy of all creepy occasions—Halloween.

Brumbaugh Hall, in the East Halls, certainly fit the descriptions--it was tall and it was a dorm. If it wasn't exactly the tallest woman's dorm in the United States, that didn't stop the story from circulating through campus. According to one report on the incident, it caused such a fever pitch that Jeanne Dixon actually wrote the Collegian explaining that the prediction had no relevance with Penn State. (It's surprising she didn't see this uproar coming.) That explanation did not stop residents of Brumbaugh Hall barricading themselves in their rooms on Halloween night, or suffering from some sleepless nights after the holiday because, you never know, maybe the murderer is a procrastinator.

The uproar wasn't restricted to the Penn State campus. The story was being kicked around like a worn hacky-sack on campuses throughout the country. It was the birth—or maybe rebirth— of an urban legend.

Snopes.com, a Web site that debunks these types of myths, classifies Penn State's Brumbaugh Massacre tale as a classic "Halloween Campus Murder" story. It's certainly not original with Penn State. The Web site speculates that stories like this were started by the true and terrifying Richard Speck murder case. Speck attacked nine nurses in a Chicago rooming house in 1966.

A few years later, the campus murder myth began to circulate in Midwestern colleges. There was a big spike in the story in 1983, just before settling in Happy Valley in 1986. In 1998, the story made its visit to American campuses again after the movie Urban Legend hit theaters.

There are other variations on the massacre theme and even some new twists, according to Snopes.com:

• In some cases, the prediction comes from that venerable prognosticator—Nostradamus.

• The psychic appears on more recent television shows—Geraldo, Oprah, and the Motel shows.

• The mass murderer can be a crazed student, mad maintenance worker, escaped convict, released mental patient, and even some nut dressed up like Little Bo Peep.

• The murder weapon is usually an axe, but can be a range of sharp objects, like a knife or a hatchet.

• The Big Ten schools that were targeted by the mass murderer included Michigan, Michigan State, Wisconsin, and Minnesota. (Maybe the suspect is an SEC fan?)

Students aren't the only ones susceptible to the campus massacre urban legend. Snopes indicates that during these rumor storms several colleges and universities inadvertently have played along, issuing warnings to students to be wary and not walk alone at night. Even though these schools assume it's better to exercise caution, these warnings only justify the story and hasten the spread of the urban legend.

Snopes.com offers an insight into the cyclical nature to the campus murder stories. The campus massacre story appears to hit in waves. The story first circulates and gains momentum. It then begins to dissipate when authorities refute the story and, hopefully, when no crazy maniac dresses as Little Bo Peep murders anyone. Those students graduate and a new crop of eager (and slightly naive) students, who have never been exposed to the story, arrive on campus. And, thus, the cycle of the urban legend continues.

Urban legend or not, back on the Penn State campus, the tale of the Brumbaugh Axe (or hatchet, or knife) Murderer continues to be passed around like the Nittany Lion is passed through the student section at Beaver Stadium. Each year, around Halloween, it's a tradition for upper-class students to have a little chat with the freshmen, especially ones who room at Brumbaugh Hall, and have a chat about psychic predictions.

They end their story with a little question: Is this the year the prediction comes true?

The Footsteps...

Old Main

Photo by George Chriss/Wikimedia Commons

Old Main serves as the focal point of the Penn State campus and a focus of some creepy legends.

Old Main is the focal point for and the administrative headquarters of Penn State's University Park campus. It was built in the shadow of the original Old Main, which was razed in 1929. The new building used some of the limestone from the original Old Main and incorporated some of its design cues.

Old Main cost a bit more than $800,000 to complete, paid by funds from state appropriations and the University's emergency building fund. Over the years, students have learned to rely on Old Main's chimes that ring out every fifteen minutes to get to class on time. On occasion, they also serve as a painful reminder of just how long a lecture is. During the week, the chimes play Westminster Quarters. On football weekends, the fight song, "The Nittany Lion," rings out from Old Main.

With its imposing facade, its long history, and solemn chimes, Old Main certainly fits the bill of a haunted building. Surely, the ghost of a former University president stalks the halls. Could a poltergeist move coffee mugs around the offices? Maybe a disgruntled student rattles office doors?

Unfortunately (or fortunately, depending how you feel about paranormal occurrences), Old Main doesn't seem to be haunted. At least, the research hasn't uncovered any stories of ghosts or spirits in the building. But, that doesn't mean that the surrounding grounds, the Old Main lawn, as it's called, hasn't stirred up some paranormal attention.

Students say there's something peculiar about the Old Main lawn. The student legend says that students should be careful at Old Main around midnight. And, students won't have any trouble determining if it is midnight; after all, the chimes toll the exact moment. Once the chimes silence, the sound of approaching footsteps can be heard. In some stories, the footsteps are soft and stealthy; in other stories, the footsteps come at you in a mad rush.

No one knows the origin of the legend and it doesn't seem to be based on a historical event.

But that doesn't stop students from taking the long way around Old Main if they're walking through campus at midnight.

The Nittany Lion: A Lesson in Cryptozoology

Penn State and all Commonwealth Campuses

Photo by Nathaniel C. Sheetz /Wikimedia Commons

The Nittany Lion Shrine is one of the most photographed sites on the Penn State campus and has become the traditional backdrop of choice of students, recent grads, alumni and guests.

Penn State's fight song, "The Nittany Lion," starts out with the lyric: "Every college has a legend..." Penn State has a collection of legends. There's a workaholic mule, an ever-vigilant house mother, and a few founders who have managed to hang around their beloved ole Penn State.

They're all treasured and beloved members of the spook-tacular alumni, but none of these famous spirits can hold a candle to the most beloved creature on the Penn State campus—the Nittany Lion. Part ferocious mountain lion, part cuddly college cub, the Nittany Lion adorns the campus. He's on posters, on shirts, and on hats. He's carved in stone and painted on walls. His paw prints are everywhere. Even on the faces of students on game day.

But, a lot of newcomers to the campus have a few questions: is the Nittany Lion real? Was there ever a pack of wild Nittany Lions that used to roam through Happy Valley? And just what the heck is a Nittany Lion anyway? Is it a cougar, or a mountain lion, or a puma, or a bobcat, or another species entirely?

The search for these answers continues to vex the most earnest crypto zoologist (someone who studies mysterious monsters and beasts).

To find the answer, we start at the very edge of Penn State history.

In the early 1800s, according to historians and naturalists, there were mountain lions that prowled Happy Valley. The mountain lion primarily subsisted on deer, rodents, birds, and, when settlers began to build farms, livestock and domesticated animals. There's no evidence to suggest that these Nittany Lions ever feasted on badgers and wolverines, despite reports to the contrary on campus.

Unfortunately, as the population boomed in Pennsylvania, the state's mountain lion prides grew scarce. The last Pennsylvania mountain lion was killed in 1856, not too long after Penn State was founded. That particular lion was preserved and is now displayed at Penn State. Originally, University officials had the lion displayed in Old Main, so that students could view it as they walked to class.

Then, they moved the mountain lion to Watts Hall where it roomed with our friend Old Coaly. The lion also was a classroom favorite, taking part in zoological classes—as an exhibit. The lion almost became a Pitt Panther, spending a few years on display in the Carnegie Museum of Natural History in Pittsburgh.

While the lion was spotted at several places on campus, his spirit was being experienced by more and more students, especially one Big Man on Campus--H.D. "Joe" Mason. In 1904 Mason and the Penn State baseball team visited Princeton for a game. Embarrassed that Princeton had a mascot--the Bengal Tiger--Mason displayed good old Penn State ingenuity--he made up a mascot. Mason said that Penn State's mascot was the Nittany Lion and the lion could easily whup up on the lowly Princeton Tiger.

Legend has it that the first of many miracles was ascribed to the Nittany Lion on that day: Penn State went on to beat Princeton's baseball team.

Mason became possessed by, or maybe obsessed with, the spirit of the lion. As a senior, Mason would later write in the student publication The Lemon, "Every college the world over of any consequence has a college emblem of some kind—all but The Pennsylvania State College. . . . Why not select for ours the king of beasts—the Lion!! Dignified, courageous, magnificent, the Lion allegorically represents all that our College Spirit should be, so why not 'the Nittany Mountain Lion?' Why cannot State have a kingly, all-conquering Lion as the eternal sentinel?"

And so, the Nittany Lion was officially adopted as the mascot.

Like all Penn State spirits, there are places on campus where his presence is more keenly felt. For most students, the place most haunted by the Nittany Lion is its shrine, located a few steps from Rec Hall, one of the school's gymnasiums and the athletic venue of choice before the Bryce Jordan Center was built.

Legendary artist Heinz Warnecke carved the lion from a thirteen-ton block of limestone. The lion is one of the most photographed—and most protected sites on campus. Back in 1966, right before the Syracuse game, the lion had been mysteriously doused with orange paint, the team colors of the Syracuse Orangemen. Suspicion was immediately placed on the Syracuse fans and the students were whipped up into a prideful fury during the game. (Later, Sue Paterno, wife of rookie coach, Joe Paterno, admitted she added a touch of easily-removed orange paint to the lion to get the students more involved in the game.)

Then, the real Syracuse fans struck. They splashed harder-to-remove orange paint on the shrine. After that, students, members of the Blue Band, professors, alumni, and even a detachment of the Penn State R.O.T.C. have made it a tradition to guard the shrine on homecoming weekend.

Pennsylvania's Bigfoot?

Most naturalists and game commission officers say that—besides the one at the sidelines and in the stands revving up the students during athletic events—there are no more mountain lions left in the central Pennsylvania area. Recently, though, sightings have made the mountain lion the "Bigfoot" of Pennsylvania. These sightings, though often anecdotal and unconfirmed, are increasing in frequency.

According to a 2006 Collegian article, the north central branch of the Pennsylvania Game Commission had close to 50 reports of mountain lion—or cougar—sightings by October of that year.

Game commissioners are adamant, these sightings are simply people misidentifying Pennsylvania's native creatures including, golden retrievers, bobcats, and even house cats. However, the state is full of ardent hunters and hikers, who are familiar with the Pennsylvania's animals. They claim they would know the difference between a golden retriever and a mountain lion, even in the thickest brush.

In 2006, there were several sightings in Bedford County. Several other mountain lions were seen by people in the Seven Mountains Area. Unfortunately, there hasn't been any hard evidence—no tracks, no pictures, and no captured animals.

There's a third explanation. Perhaps there are mountain lions in Pennsylvania, they're just not natives. The game commission speculates that a cougar or two could have been held illegally and escaped. It would be the first time.

Recently, the game commission points out, a binturong was found on a Beaver County family's porch. A native of Southeast Asia, a binturong is also known as a bearcat. The bearcat didn't swim from Vietnam; it was probably illegally possessed by someone and it escaped.

Just like the debate over the existence of Bigfoot, the argument about Pennsylvania's Bigfoot—the mountain lion—will rage on for some time. But mountain lion believers and scientists do agree on one thing. The mountain lion population is rebounding. Confirmed sightings have for the first time been registered east of the Mississippi. Most biologists say that Pennsylvania could make good "cat country" with plentiful deer and other game to feed on.

How long will it be before the Nittany Lion's roar will pierce the wilds of Happy Valley once again.

Penn State's Haunted Hot Spots

Favorite haunted bars, taverns, pubs, and hangouts

Penn State students don't spend all their time attending lectures in haunted buildings and studying in poltergeist-filled dorm rooms. They've been known to frequent the bars and taverns in State College's downtown and surrounding areas, especially after a week of studying for exams, writing papers, and updating their Facebook accounts.

It seems that wherever the students go, tales of ghosts and spirits follow closely behind and the old Penn State haunts are no different.

The best place to start the search for spots that have spirits… with spirits… is downtown State College.

State College is the community that grew up with the University. Once it was nothing more than a few streets and a couple stores that served the needs of the small group of students who attended the college for farmers. Now, it's a busy little city with apartment buildings, packed streets, and a sprawling assortment of bars and taverns to suit the tastes of students.

Some of those bars just happen to be haunted, according to local legends.

Skeller Rats and Spirits with Spirits

The All American Rathskeller

It's been said that if Bluto and the rest of the *Animal House* gang went to Penn State, it's an even bet that they'd log some time— probably a lot of time—hanging out in one of State College's favorite bars: the Rathskeller.

The Rathskeller, or Skeller for those in the know, was created right after the end of Prohibition. And we mean right after Prohibition. When Congress ended the ban on the selling and imbibing of booze on Nov. 6, 1933, a neon light went on over local restaurateur "Pop" Flood's head. In just three days, Pop, who owned the Green Room Restaurant, opened the Rathskeller and Gardens.

When Pop got an idea, he didn't waste any time. The Rathskeller was the fourth licensed bar in the state. The subterranean bar quickly became a popular hangout for college students, too.

There were a lot of Pennsylvania businesses getting into the spirit of post-Prohibition innovations. A brewery was opening up in Latrobe, Pa., called Rolling Rock. Pop figured it would be a natural fit and a sign of Keystone State solidarity to sell Rolling Rock beer at his establishment and another tradition was born. The Rock Pony, or a Rolling Rock pony bottle, is the brew of choice for Penn State students at the Skeller.

Just a year later, the Floods sold the bar to concentrate on their restaurant business. The new owner, C.C. "Doggie" Alexander, changed the name to the All-American Rathskeller. But the Rathskeller tradition—and the Rathskeller tradition of creating traditions—lived on.

In 1965, Doggie passed on. But current staff and patrons still pay homage to his friendly spirit in the bar. It's reported that when the staff locks the door at another great night end of the night of Skeller revelry, the workers will often whisper, "Goodnight, Doggie."

It's not just the owners who haunt this establishment. Former patrons have etched their own spirit into the fabric of the Skeller. Some have passed on, but today's patrons say you can still feel their presence.

In the old Skeller days, people who hung around the bar—or worked there—were given a new title. A "Skeller Rat" is a high title for staff and patrons. One of the most famous Skeller Rats was Harry Frank Neideigh. According to the Skeller's website, Harry came into the Skeller in 1948, ordered two pony bottles and, pretty much, never left. He worked at the University, in the dining halls. But he'd rather serve brews to the students than food.

Harry loved the Skeller so much that even though he hadn't been on the payroll since the early 1960s, he showed up regularly. He would set up for lunch, turn on the neon light and check out the Bloody Mary mix before the weekend football festivities. When he wasn't volunteering, he'd sit in his favorite seat and watch his favorite shows, the *Price is Right* and *All My Children*... and do a little girl watching, too.

During his stint at the Skeller, Harry has seen a lot of students come and go and has out-lasted at least four owners, according to the website. In fact, Harry was usually part of the sales agreement. Before an owner signed the bottom line, he or she had to take care of Harry.

In 2001, Harry passed away. His barmates say he went on to the light and, knowing Harry, it was a neon one.

There are some students and Skeller Rats who say that Harry hasn't left entirely. A slew of stories have filtered out of the below-ground-level bar about some paranormal activities. For some witnesses, it's a sense that there's a presence, or a feeling that you're not alone. Most put their bets on Harry.

He seems like he would have the most motive for lingering in his favorite bar. Others say it's the ghost of one of the founding owners, Doggie.

Another camp claims that the spirit that haunts the Rathskeller is a negative energy. They believe that a tragic incident that occurred outside the bar may have something to do with the odd feelings people have when they're alone. In a fight between bouncers and a student, a student died. People speculate that this is the source of the Rathskeller's haunting.

There are still others that believe the Rathskeller, which is a pretty old building, is haunted by much older spirit. Unfortunately, no one is sure when the haunting began. Indeed, the bar is a memorial to those past spirits. Photos of past owners, old customers, and former employees litter the hangout.

According to a Collegian article, the Skeller's most recent owner called members of the Penn State Paranormal Research Society to investigate it. The team brought in recorders to check for electronic voice phenomenon (EVPs), cameras for capturing spirits on film, and other high-tech paranormal investigation equipment.

Whether the Penn State PRS team, or anyone else for that matter, will be able to solve the Skeller mystery is a matter of debate at the All American Rathskeller. And, as long as there's a fresh supply of Rolling Rock pony bottles, it probably always will.

In Memoriam...

Duffy's Tavern, Boalsburg

While State College grew from a small college town to a thriving community woven into the resources of a Big Ten research institution, Boalsburg, a small town a few miles outside State College, has retained that old college town feel. Boalsburg has an artsy, academic feel and continues to relish its traditions and history.

Remembering and honoring the dead are among those cherished traditions. Boalsburg is one of the communities credited with initiating the Memorial Day holiday. The story goes that in 1864, three local women, who were grievously hard hit by the raging Civil War, went to the cemetery where their fallen loved ones rested. The meeting between the women was random.

Gettysburg was a recent memory for the women. Some of the most ferocious fighting was just a few months away.

They placed flowers on the graves and talked. The day would have been uneventful save for the promise the three women made to each other as they left the cemetery. They promised to meet at the graveyard again next year. The random meeting of three women grew to an annual tradition of memorializing the dead.

There are several communities who claim the tradition of the first Memorial Day, but Boalsburg has adopted the day as its own. The community holds a Memorial Day celebration each year with food, crafts, music, parades, and athletic events. The Pennsylvania Military Museum, also located in Boalsburg, is the fulcrum of events for the holiday.

But the military museum and local cemeteries aren't the only places to find a reverence for spirits.

Duffy's Tavern, located in the center of Boalsburg in a district called "the diamond," is one of the most popular eateries t for Penn State students and faculty. It's also reportedly pretty popular with the spirit world.

The tavern was built in 1819 and served the needs of travelers on the stagecoaches that passed through the area. Some say that the architecture of the building hints at spiritual activity. Two sharply-angled windows, some say, were installed to keep out evil spirits. (Although no one said anything about keep good spirits in....)

Harry Duffy, an owner who passed away in 1961, made sure the tavern was clean, friendly and, of course, offered good food. The current restaurant continues to uphold that colonial hospitality like Harry never left.

And, maybe, Harry Duffy never did.

Customers and staff members have been passing on stories about a ghost at Duffy's Tavern for years. Harry is the prime suspect, though some suggest the building has more than one spirit traveler.

Like a good restaurant owner, Harry offers a complete buffet of paranormal behavior. According to a Collegian article, Harry often manifests as a *presence* or a feeling when the employee is alone.

But, he's been known to show up on occasion. Patrons have reported seeing a ghost floating around the dining room.

Other stories seem to show off Harry's penchant for practical jokes. Once, employees arrived at the restaurant to set up for a banquet. When they entered the room, they were shocked to discover all of the chairs that were once lined up perfectly, were now arranged in a circle. More puzzling, the banquet room had been locked and no staff members or customers had been in the room since the night before.

According to the Daily Collegian article, the daughter of the tavern's owner and a long-time Duffy's Tavern employee said she went to check the restaurant on Christmas Day. To her shock, the water was running in all of the sinks. She was sure they had been shut off before and no one had been in the restaurant.

Other reports of poltergeist-like behavior include latched doors that suddenly snap open and then slam shut. Glasses—that are well beyond the grasp of even the clumsiest bartender—have been known to cascade off the bar.

Staff members are quick to point out that Harry isn't malicious. Most of his stunts are more like practical jokes that he pulls when he needs more attention. Like any good-natured prankster, Harry will even lay-off the joking, if he's asked nicely. Once, while a bartender was fielding questions about whether Harry was real or not from a group of customers, when the lights inexplicably turned off.

The bartender told Harry to knock it off... and the lights immediately turned back on, as the customers sat stunned.

Living for Evermore

The Eutaw House, Potters Mills

Just a few miles beyond Penn State, as the raven flies, is an area called Poe Valley. Poe Valley is an isolated strip of wilderness that is surrounded by the Bald Eagle State Park. Since the valley was tagged with the last name of arguably America's great writer of horror, legends of the area's connection with Edgar Allan Poe pulse through the valley.

One legend is that the area was named after a relative of Poe's and that, in fact, Poe ventured there to settle the estate when this relative died. He fell in love with the place. The solemn, steep mountains dotted by lonesome pines, maples and oak disappear into the pointed fingers of dark valleys that seem to hold time in their shadowy grip. It's no wonder that the master of the macabre felt right at home.

The legend also says that he was so inspired by Poe Valley that he wrote *The Raven*, his most famous poem, while he stayed at the nearby inn, The Eutaw House.

As evidence, believers point to the flocks of ravens that hang out near Poe Valley and the Eutaw House. Were these the winged inspiration for the moody writer to create, *The Raven*, which has been called the most perfect poem in literature?

There's still more evidence. On a Eutaw House table, there's a curious etching. Carved in the table are three letters: E. A. P. Could it be that Poe scratched his initials into the wood as a memento of the occasion—or perhaps just another example of his rebellious soul? There are lots of believers who think so.

Those who believe in the Eutaw House-Poe connection say the writer etched more than his initials into the Eutaw House; his spirit is also eternally enshrined in the hotel and restaurant. People say the ghost of Poe is the cause of the haunted happenings at the Eutaw House.

Witnesses have reported seeing a thin man with dark hair and a mustache walking the halls of the Eutaw House. In a flash, he disappears. The figure looked a lot like Edgar Allan Poe, the witnesses add.

But, Poe, who lived a lonely existence, has plenty of company in the afterlife. The Eutaw House, they say, is packed with other spirits and stories of ghosts.

The hotel was ideally situated as a resting spot for travelers and stagecoach riders. Not all the travelers journeyed on, at least in an earthly sense. One of the visiting groups that spent the night at the Eutaw House was a wagon-load of inmates from a nearby jail. Legend has it that one of the prisoners escaped and hanged himself in the inn's attic. Ever since this incident, his disturbing presence has been felt and perhaps experienced as poltergeist-like phenomenon. Several incidents of moved furniture and disturbed rooms have been reported. In some cases, these events happened when no one was around; at other times, witnesses watched as dishes moved on their own and trays were pushed off tables.

Some ascribe other paranormal activity to the Eutaw House poltergeist. Anomalous activities and electromagnetic phenomenon, such as lights and televisions turning on and off by themselves, occur regularly.

The Hanging

Another misfortune happened when a Native American, who was accused of stealing horses, was captured near the inn. In those days, vigilante justice was more often meted out as the preferred form of justice. The accused thief was dragged to a tree and hanged on the spot.

The sound of the grisly act is now repeated over and over like a paranormal broken record. Guests have reported that while staying overnight in the inn they have heard the unmistakable snap of a rope, the heavy thud of a body hitting something solid—like a tree—and the creak.

The Lady in Black

A hub of paranormal activity is at the inn's central staircase. People have claimed to see the ghost of a woman dressed in black and a young girl at this staircase, or on the stairs.

Since the woman appears to be dressed in funeral clothes, her spirit is tied to another ghost—the ghost of a crying young girl. Those who witnessed the apparition think that the woman is crying for her dead daughter.

But that's not the only place ghosts are seen at the Eutaw House. Reports filter in from all over the inn. For instance, the three figures—the woman, the child, and the ghost of the man who looks like Poe—are seen both inside the Eutaw House and walking the grounds. Have these souls connected in the after-life?

Guests say that despite the haunted history of the Eutaw House they have never feared for their lives, nor has anyone ever felt threatened by the ghosts.

The spirits seem friendly, they say.

And possibly very poetic.

Gone (Again), but Not Forgotten

Gatsby's, former downtown nightclub

Students who went to Penn State in the 1980s often spent Friday and Saturday nights digging local musicians at a place called Gatsby's.

The nightclub was known for good times, good food, good drinks and a ghost named George. George, so the story went, was an employee of the movie house that occupied the building long before the bar opened. George died in the mid-1950s, at least that's when reports of a mysterious man lurking around the movie theater began to surface.

When the nightclub came into existence the paranormal party really started to hop. George was seen by dozens of customers, staff members, and visitors. Granted, some of these reports came from patrons who were enjoying some of the great drink specials available at Gatsby's. If those folks were the only sources of George sightings, the haunting could easily be dismissed; but they weren't.

George was seen by at least two managers—stone sober, no-nonsense business types. Those sightings added a more respectable twist to the Gatsby's haunting and the spirit's reputation began to grow. The best times for stories about George were around Halloween, of course. During the Halloween season, the bar was filled with whispered anecdotes of possible George sightings, tales of paranormal encounters, and questions about the origin of the ghost.

Unfortunately, the big 80s came to an end in State College. Hair became a little tamer. Metal music turned to grunge. And for Gatsby patrons and, probably, George, the end of the 80s was the end of the line for their favorite bar. In 1989, the bar was closed and Penn State bought the building.

Penn State renamed it the Scott Building and it currently serves as an annex for the University's English Department.

Since then, George hasn't been sighted around the newly-christened English annex. Paranormal experts are stumped.

Maybe he just moved to the fiction department.

Branch Campus Spirits

The Uncommonly Spooky Sites On and Near Penn State's Commonwealth Campuses

Penn State isn't just one school; it's a network of centers for learning. During the Depression, Penn State leaders spread the educational opportunities across the Commonwealth to make sure all students had access to a college education.

The 24 commonwealth campuses are often referred to as "branch campuses."

They were once mainly two-year "prep" schools that allowed students to begin their college careers close to home and then complete their degrees at the main campus in University Park.

Things have changed. These campuses now boast just as many amenities as the main campus. Like Penn State at University Park campus, these schools offer four-year degrees, state-of-the-art facilities, athletic teams, academic clubs, and, as you might have guessed, stories about campus ghosts.

Penn State Altoona

Ghost of the Buckhorn, Railroad Spirits

Located in a wooded nook on the outskirts of Altoona, Pa., Penn State Altoona is often described as the jewel of Penn State's Commonwealth Campuses.

Over the years, it's grown from the seed of an idea germinated by a group of Altoona business men and women, who wanted to create a center for undergraduate education in the Altoona area. In 1939, they went with their idea to then Penn State President Ralph Hetzel. The citizens then embarked on a fundraising campaign to seed the project. Within a few months, the $5,000 was raised and the center took shape in an abandoned elementary school building. The school started with a little over 100 students. It now has over 3800 students and offers 18 bachelor's degrees.

Penn State Altoona also offers a chance for students to explore the haunted landscape of central Pennsylvania. The school is conveniently located near several paranormal spots.

Lady of the Buckhorn

Penn State Altoona lies at the foot of the Wopsononock Mountain--nicknamed "Wopsy" by students. Juniata Gap Road, which passes the campus, winds its way up the mountain and the adjoining Buckhorn Mountain. It's a twisty, narrow mountain road that students have been known to drive, often to explore the place that spawned the legend of the Lady of the Buckhorn. And, occasionally to explore its reputation as a lover's lane.

In either case, the Lady of the Buckhorn—or the Lady in White—is arguably Altoona's best-known legend.

There are several variations.

Usually, it begins with a couple on a drive to the Buckhorn. (They're usually a Penn State Altoona campus couple looking for the lover's lane.)

During the drive, they spy a woman standing at the side of the road. She's dressed in a white gown that flutters in the Wopsy breeze. In some cases, she's expressionless; in other stories, she looks sad and hopeless. Sometimes, she has a lantern; other times, she has a candle in her hands.

As the car passes the woman, the driver checks the rear-view mirror. When he does, he's startled to see that the lady has disappeared!

But when the passenger turns to look out the back window, the Lady in White is sitting, serenely, in the back seat. Typically, she makes no effort to communicate.

Once the car rounds a severe curve called, appropriately enough, *the Devil's Elbow*, the lady disappears, leaving the couple dumbfounded and—as if it needs to be mentioned—scared out of their wits.

The identity of the Lady of the Buckhorn is a bit of a mystery. Like most urban legends, she doesn't seem to be a historical figure. There are lots of explanations and these variations indicate the age of this legend. In some early versions, the woman was thrown from a buggy. In others, she was a victim of a car accident. The ghost might not be a woman at all. There are people who believe it was a baby that died on the Buckhorn and her spirit, who has now assumed the form of her grown-up self, is the phantom passenger. Still other believers in the tale suggest the lady is the mother of the deceased child.

There is also considerable speculation as to why she paranormally hitchhikes on the Buckhorn late at night, but these stories follow the well-trodden path of the urban legend: take a happy couple, add a misfortune, and that adds up to a haunting

The most popular version of how the White Lady's haunting began reads like a ridge runner Romeo and Juliette story and goes something like this:

Despite an ongoing feud between their families, a man and a woman met and fell in love. Knowing that they could never live in peace, they decided to elope and leave Altoona. And the only way to leave Altoona, they thought, was to drive over the Buckhorn.

In those days, the Buckhorns turns were only frequented by the hell-raisers and moonshiners called ridge runners, who used the curvy roads to elude the police. The couple reasoned that family members, if they gave chase, would never be able to catch them.

Catch them alive, at least.

Initially, the plan goes well. The man drove to the woman's house, flicked the headlights on three times, turned off the engine and coasts passed the house. He looks at the house and the porch light is turned on and off—three times.

The signal!

Seconds later, the woman darts through the shadow and jumps into the car. They speed away.

But there was one fatal flaw in the plan. The woman tells her sister what the couple plans to do. Facing an irate father, the sister breaks down and tells him everything.

The father chases after them and, as the couple's vehicle starts the long, twisted ascent up the Buckhorn, the beau nervously eyes the rapidly-approaching headlights in his rear-view mirror.

"It's my father!" the woman shouts and the man tromps his foot on the gas.

He tries to put distance between his car and the father's car. Tires squeal through the tight turns. Nothing seems to work. The father remains on the couple's trail. It's like a demon is following him.

The man drives even faster, as he approaches the Devil's Elbow.

Too fast, it turns out.

The man can't hold the car on the road and loses control. The car flies off the road and into a tree.

The woman dies instantly.

Since then, the Lady in White returns to the spot of the accident, searching for her lost love.

At least that's one story...

Other Paranormal Spots in Altoona

For the paranormally-inclined students, there are other opportunities for ghost hunting—or scaring some classmates—in Altoona. It's arguably one of the most haunted spots in central Pennsylvania. (Penn State's main campus is its closest competition.)

Several sites have garnered enough attention to draw in the crew from Sci-Fi's Ghost Hunters for an investigation.

The Mishler Theater was one of the Altoona spots explored by the show and continues to be a source of great ghost stories of the students of

Penn State Altoona. The grand theater, which attracted the brightest stars of vaudeville, like Al Jolson and George Burns, was built in 1906.

At the insistence of its creator, Isaac Mishler, the building was the area's grandest theater, although maybe not the luckiest. Just a few months after it was opened, a nearby building caught fire. The blaze spread and engulfed the Mishler. A year later, the theater was re-built.

Isaac Mishler has proven to be just as persistent in death as he was in life, especially when it comes to his beloved theater. Isaac is one of the spirits that people claim to see hanging around the theater. He's usually seen in fleeting glimpses.

A few people have had more than the fleeting interaction, though.

One woman said when her mother, a worker at the Mishler, used to take her to the theater. She was allowed to occupy herself as her mother worked. The theater was a fun place to explore, but it was also pretty spooky at times. Luckily, while searching through the theater, an older man befriended her and escorted her.

When she told her mother about the encounter, her mother became unnerved. There shouldn't be anyone in the theater at the time. So, her mother asked for a description. As the girl described the man, it became pretty clear that the older gentleman was Isaac Mishler.

Mr. Mishler isn't involved in a one man show at the theater; he reportedly has an entire cast with him at the theater. The supporting spirits include a lady who wears 1930s-era garb and the ghost of a young man.

Altoona Railroaders Museum

Across the train tracks from the Mishler Theater is the Altoona Railroaders museum. At one time, Altoona was the hub of train traffic in the northeast.

The Altoona Railroaders Museum, which occupies the former Penn Central Railroad shop complex, is now the hub of paranormal activity.

The main ghost in the museum is called "Frank" by his admirers. He has been seen by several visitors to the museum, staff members, and even museum officials. The descriptions are similar and resemble one of the men in a 1920s-era picture of railroad workers that hangs in the museum.

Baker Mansion

Students at Penn State Altoona aren't opposed to hitting the dance floor every once and awhile. They might prefer their dance partner actually have a head... and torso... and legs, though.

The Baker Mansion, a stately Greek Revival mansion, is now a museum. It was built in 1849 by iron mogul Elias Baker. There are those that believe the mansion is stately and magnificent. Others agree it's stately, maybe; but, austere and cold are better adjectives. It looks, well, sort of like a mausoleum.

While aesthetic opinions vary, no one disagrees that Baker Mansion is big and that's a lucky thing. The mansion needs all that extra room to house the many wandering spirits trapped behind its stately—or cold—walls.

One of the treasured objects on display is an old wedding dress. There's also a story that goes along with it. Anna, the daughter of the mansion's owner, was engaged to be married. But, Anna never got the chance to wear it. Anna fell in love with a common worker and Elias would not allow the marriage. Eventually, he got his way, but Anna never married. Ann died in the mansion—alone.

Years later, the wedding dress of another mogul's daughter was displayed in the mansion. It was a hit with visitors to the museum. Not everyone liked it.

On full moons, some say the dress dances. Other witnesses aren't so sure: they think the glass case is being shaken by someone—or something—so hard that the dress appears to be dancing, but it's not doing a happy dance. These witnesses theorize that Anna is upset that someone would put a reminder of a happy wedding, something she never experienced.

The ghosts of Elias and son, Sylvester have also been seen in the mansion. Another suspected Baker Mansion spook is the Baker's son, David. David was killed in a steamboat accident and was brought back to the mansion for burial. When his body arrived a brutal Pennsylvania weather had set in and the ground was frozen hard. Since the family had nowhere to store the body, the Bakers kept David's body in the cellar.

The Baker family made a series of missteps if they wanted to avoid; storing a dead body in the basement was probably the worst one.

It's almost like they tried to own Altoona's most haunted mansion.

Col. Wiestling and the Sadie's Ghost

Penn State Mont Alto

Penn State Mont Alto merged with the Penn State system in 1929. At the time, the Pennsylvania State Forestry School, as the school was then called, was one of the nation's premiere forestry schools.

Let's just say, the merger wasn't the happiest in Penn State history.

If there's one spirit that pervades the Mont Alto campus, it's a rebel spirit. Maybe because the campus lies so close to some of America's greatest Civil War battlefields, like Harper's Ferry, Gettysburg, and Antietam, the fire of rebellion stoked the students of the forestry school when they heard about the merger.

And hell broke loose.

The students hanged members of the state legislature who ordered the merger in effigy outside of their dorms. Students then held a rally and created a huge bonfire that was attended by thousands of people from the small community. Reports of the event covered the entire front page of the local newspaper.

The flames of the bonfire eventually died down and so did that rebellious spirit. But not all the spirits of Mont Alto are willing to fade into the past. Mont Alto is one of the most paranormally active commonwealth campuses.

One of the best places for a supernatural encounter at Mont Alto is at Wiestling Hall. It's no wonder the student center is haunted: the hall is reportedly the oldest building in the Penn State system. Naturally, the connection with Col. George Wiestling, an ironmaster and one of Mont

Alto's founding citizens, only enhances the building's haunted pedigree. Wiestling lived in the home for several years.

At one time, Wiestling oversaw the Mont Alto Iron Works, a sprawling site that employed over 500 people. The iron works was dismantled and sold to the Pennsylvania State Forestry Commission, which then turned it into the forestry school.

When students began to use the building, they noticed strange things. First, there were knocks. Students claimed to have heard loud bangs on doors and sometimes walls.

Then, students said the Colonel would go for a stroll. His footsteps would echo through the building.

Poltergeist activity—objects moving and disappearing—is often blamed on the Colonel, too. When the building was used as a dining hall, food service workers bore the brunt of the Colonel's tricks. On one occasion, a potato-peeling machine turned on, all by itself. In another incident, pots and pans were heard clanging together, even though no one was in the room at the time. Students who worked at Wiestling usually had their own stories. One student was asked to move two tables. He went to get help. When he came back, one table was leaned on top of the other table.

There's also a mysterious class picture. Those who have seen the 1908 Class photo say that there is a blurry shape posing with the group. Has Col. Wiestling been captured on film?

The Sad Spirit Named Sadie

Paranormal experts say that the Colonel is joined in his home by the sad ghost of murder victim. According to the story, in 1911 Sadie Hurley, who worked in the food hall, was shot several times by William Reed, her boyfriend. Sadie was still alive when help arrived. She was taken inside the hall and up the steps to the attic, where she eventually died.

When he was arrested, Reed claimed it was an accidental shooting. He said he went to see her to get some papers and only pulled the gun to scare her.

The court didn't buy the flimsy excuse. He was hanged for murder in Chambersburg, the last man to be hanged there for a crime.

Whether it had any connection to the incident or not, the attic has reportedly never been refurbished and it can only be accessed by two hidden doors.

Sadie reportedly still haunts the attic. Noises in the area are attributed to the restless spirit of the murder victim.

A few brave students have snuck up to the attic, armed with flashlights and curiosity. Students say flashlights almost immediately grow dim and then go out. Then, the students claim to hear the rapid beat of footsteps coming toward them and then bid a hasty retreat.

Paranormal investigators would say that the spiritual energies are gnawing out the power of the flashlights; an occurrence that is common in haunted spots.

Mont Alto has other placed for students with an interest in the paranormal to explore. Next to Wiestling Hall, the most famous haunted spot on the Mont Alto campus is Mont Alto Hall.

In a Collegian article, a student claimed that the dorm is haunted by a previous resident. The resident was electrocuted and died in her room. Now, the legend states the scent of smoke fills dorm rooms.

Dorm RAs have been called in to investigate and usually come up empty.

Poor, Frozen Henry

Penn State Erie, The Behrend College

The Spring Semester is a bit of a misnomer at Penn State Erie, the Behrend College. It's anything but spring-like during the early part of the spring semester.

In January, the winds whip across Lake Erie, dropping the wind chill factor into the sub-zero range and depositing massive amounts of snow on the Penn State Erie campus. The winds aren't the only things whipping around the Penn State Erie campus; stories about the ghost of a student named Henry blow around campus, especially during those frigid months of the so-called Spring Semester.

The story goes something like this: In the 1970s, a student, known only as Henry, was staying in the west wing of the school's Niagara Hall at Penn State Erie. The school was donated to Penn State in 1948 by Mary Behrend, whose husband co-founded the Hammermill Paper Company. In 1973, maybe around the time Henry was attending, Penn State's board of trustees granted four-year and graduate college status to Penn State Behrend, the first commonwealth campus in the Penn State system to achieve that status.

Henry lived on the third floor of the Niagara, named after the flagship commanded by Commodore Perry in his victory over the British during the Battle of Lake Erie.

During one, particularly cold winter night, Henry suffered a string of misfortunes that caused his death. First, the heating unit in his dorm room broke. The cold temperatures also jammed his doors and windows shut. He tried desperately to shout for help, but those pleas went unanswered.

When his roommate arrived the next morning, he found Henry slumped over the non-working heater. He froze to death.

On some nights—especially cold nights—residents say you can still hear Henry shaking the heater, trying to bring the equipment back to life. Doors and windows have also been known to shake on the nights when Henry is active, too. Perhaps, it's a grim reenactment of Henry's frantic fight for life.

There might be another explanation. Henry might just be a construction of dorm residents' collective imaginations. Henry might even be a less-than-subtle complaint to members of the physical plant that their rooms are too cold on those winter nights. It's a college way to say, "turn up the heat!"

Real person or a veiled complaint, Henry may have served a purpose. On the Penn State Behrend web site, there's a list of improvements the school made to Niagara Hall in 2004, among them: new sprinklers, ceiling tiles, lighting, roof, and carpeting. More importantly, the heating units in the student bedrooms were replaced.

So Henry can now rest (warmly) in peace.

Mad Ghosts

Penn State Brandywine

It's not intentional, but Penn State founders have an odd habit of inviting the paranormal into their campuses.

They placed a grave in the middle of the University Park campus.

They turned a haunted ironmaster's mansion and murder scene into a dining hall in Mont Alto.

And, in 1967, they created what is now Penn State Brandywine just four miles from the Brandywine Battlefield, site of one of the largest battles in the American Revolution and reportedly a pretty active paranormal site.

It's a favorite topic among believers and skeptics alike on the Penn State Brandywine campus. Most of the ghost stories that pervade the battlefield site are about American Revolution hero, General "Mad" Anthony Wayne. Gen. Wayne got the nickname "mad" because of his quick temper.

Back on Sept. 11, 1777, as British troops skillfully maneuvered around colonial troops at the Brandywine Creek near Chadd's Ford, General Wayne had something to be mad about. The loss of the battle of Brandywine allowed the British to seize Philadelphia, the capital of the colonial government at the time.

Brandywine has since become an epicenter for hauntings in the area. Two area inns, The General Wayne Inn and the General Warren Inn, are said to be haunted. The battlefield itself has been the scene of a few ghostly sightings. Photographers have reported "orb" phenomenon. When they take a picture, strange anomalies, like round balls of light, appear in the picture.

It could be the energy—and maybe the disappointment—of the intense battle has imprinted itself on the fabric of reality in this space, just a few miles from the Penn State Brandywine campus.

Step Back Coaly, Here's Old Duke

Penn State Greater Allegheny

Old Coaly and the Nittany Lion have a little competition for students' love on the campus of Penn State Greater Allegheny. For years, a huge white-tailed buck roamed the campus, which was then called Penn State McKeesport, located just less than 20 miles away from Pittsburgh.

Students nicknamed the buck, Duke. There was something special about Duke. He usually sported a massive, sixteen-point antler rack. He was also bigger than the average deer and Duke roamed the campus like the Big Man on Campus.

There was one other strange thing about Duke. He was an unlikely transfer student; the campus is a little too urban of a setting for a deer.

In any event, Duke's enrollment lasted about 16 years. When the body of a massive stag—with a 16-point rack—was discovered in the fields just outside of campus, students and staff thought it would be the last time they would see Duke.

They were wrong.

Since Duke's passing, students and staff continue to catch fleeting glimpse of a large buck. In some of those reports, the deer has the unmistakable antler with sixteen points.

The Beaver Campus Lady in White

Penn State Beaver

Penn State Beaver is a 100-acre campus that's conveniently situated about half-hour from downtown Pittsburgh.

Before Penn State Beaver became a refuge for learning, it was a refuge for the sick and dying. In 1965, the Beaver County Board of Commissioners offered the University the old county hospital buildings and grounds for use as a Commonwealth campus.

During the tuberculosis outbreak that devastated the country, the county hospital served as a sanatorium. When tuberculosis victims came to the hospital, it was rarely for treatment; it was a place for them to die in relative peace. Tuberculosis, a disease that most commonly attacked the lungs, was an equal opportunity illness; it struck the old and the young, and the rich and the poor. It was a slow and agonizing death. Those who worked at the tuberculosis sanatoriums and those who miraculously survived their stays report that death was omnipresent--thousands were said to have died at the Beaver County facility.

For those who were in the prime of their lives, the effect of tuberculosis was particularly devastating. They clung to life with every minute, with every difficult breath. Office workers who now inhabit the administration buildings have stories that indicate some are still clinging, unable to transcend the thin veil that separates life from death.

In some cases, workers hear footsteps. In the spookiest stories, workers who are in the building late hear footsteps coming toward their offices from a distance. The crisp echoes of the footsteps come close and closer, until they resound in the same office and stop right in front of their desk or workspace. Then, the worker has a sensation like someone is watching, waiting. It's an unnerving moment.

For one worker, a nurse, it wasn't just footsteps or a haunted feeling; she encountered the real thing—a full body apparition and possibly even some contact. The nurse came forward with her story to a television crew, saying that on one occasion as she walked down the hall, she looked into a lounge. When she passed, she saw a young lady with long blonde hair looking out the windows onto the campus grounds. Initially, she thought it was a student or a member of the staff; but it was late and she had through she was alone. When she noticed the lady wore a white dressing gown, she knew something was amiss. The nurse was filled with a mixture of fear and incredible sadness. She walked away.

But, the Lady in White would return to the nurse. Once, she even heard the ghost say her name. Another time, as she entered the old administration building, she looked into a basement window. Staring back at her were two eyes. No face. Just the eyes.

Despite her scientific background and her own religious beliefs that discounted a belief in the paranormal, the nurse began to investigate her encounters. Older citizens of the town verified several elements of her story, including one elderly lady who said she not only saw the ghost of the Lady in White, she at one time played with her when she was living.

The nurse also discovered that the basement—the same place where the faceless eyes stared out at her--was the place where bodies were stored before they could be properly buried.

It's understandable why the spirit—or spirits—became so attached to the nurse. The nurses in the sanatorium were the hands of caring and understanding during their struggle with life. Now, it seems that the spirits are again reaching out to the nurses for understanding; this time, however, it's to help them with their struggle with death.

Lights. Cameras. Spirits?

Penn State Fayette, The Eberly Campus

At first glance, most students who arrive at Penn State Fayette would guess that the relatively new campus and pastoral setting would be the last place they would find a ghost.

They're probably right. There doesn't seem to be much paranormal activity at Penn State Fayette, but that didn't stop filmmakers from making it the setting of a horror film. The campus was used as one of the locations used in the filming of "George A. Romero Presents... Deadtime Stories," an anthology of horror stories in 2007. The one shot at Penn State Fayette was called, "Dust" and was the story.

Romero, of course, is a legend in the horror film legend. Jeff Monahan, a director from the nearby town of Connellsville, Pa., partnered with Romero on the idea.

It's a good bet that Monahan recognized the spooky power that college campuses exude when he decided on a Penn State location for the movie.

The Ancient and the Restless

Near Penn State Schuylkill

The grounds around Penn State Schuylkill have a long history, a somewhat sad history, and, according to some, a haunted history.

Penn State Schuylkill is located in Schuylkill Haven, a small town situated between Allentown and Harrisburg. When Penn State decided to build a campus--or a center, as they were called at the time—they found a site that's history was planted into the mid-18th century.

In the terms of paranormal real estate, founders couldn't have asked for better haunted potential. According to campus history, there was a self-supporting almshouse, a hospital, a building for "the insane, distraught, and poor," and a morgue.

Despite the enticing paranormal possibilities, there isn't a lot of activity on campus; at least, no one has stepped forward to admit it. However, over the hill from the campus is Rest Haven, a rest home for the aged and infirmed.

Local paranormal investigators and historians say this spot is haunted. The stories that filtered out of Rest Haven indicate that there are several apparitions: the ghost of a woman, a man, and an undertaker.

These are ghost stories with a supernatural twist, though. While most ghosts are content with conducting their residual business; at least two of the ghosts are on a mission. One nurse said she walked past a room at night and noticed a man next to the bed of a woman. Since visiting hours were over, the nurse asked the man to leave. The nurse then walked away, but some unsettled feeling led her back to the woman's room. When she returned, she discovered the man was gone; but so was the patient. She had apparently died soon after the woman died, leaving the nurse to speculate was this dark figure some sort of harbinger of death.

Another spirit that haunts Rest Haven is the ghost of an Amish man. Residual in nature, the man, who is dressed in black and wears a wide-brimmed hat, is seen walking down the stairs to the old morgue. He probably doesn't have to worry about anyone following him.

Penn State Schuylkill students who want to have more campus ghost stories might be in for a treat; there have been indications that Penn State may be interested in adding the Rest Haven grounds to the campus.

It should make Halloweens more interesting at Penn State Schuylkill.

A Bridge Too Far Out?

Penn State Berks

The town of Reading is another place in Pennsylvania with an extensive haunted background. Paranormal experts familiar with the hauntings say that the spirits in Reading may be a bit more active than the normal Penn State spooks—and a bit more aggressive.

The spirit life of Reading is filled with stories of demonic intrusions and tales of suicides. Stories about people who end their lives by jumping off of bridges are a particularly popular theme in Reading's folk tales. Penn State Berks just happens to be one bridge away from this haunted territory and some of the spirits appear to be slowly branching out from Haunted Reading.

Penn State Berks, located in Wyomissing, Pa., started out as Wyomissing Polytechnic Institute. The Institute was headquartered in a building that was formerly the Sacred Heart Church. In 1958, WMI became the Penn State Wyomissing Center, but it moved in 1972 to its present location that straddles the banks of Tulpehocken Creek.

As creeks go, Tulpehocken Creek isn't much to talk about, but for Penn State Berks students who have an affinity for the paranormal, the creek is more than the campus border, it's a watery demarcation line between the natural and the supernatural.

Students say the easiest way to cross over this void is to take a walk across a covered bridge that straddles Tulpehocken Creek, preferably after dark. The bridge—sometimes called the Red Bridge or Wertz's Bridge—is close to the campus and is one of Berks County's famous covered bridges. According to student legend it's more infamous than famous. One student legend says that a mother tossed her children off the bridge before she killed herself. The negative residual energy remains on the campus, the legend goes on to say. There are also accounts of strange noises at the bridge at night.

Skeptics point out that the legend has its obvious problems. To begin with, the covered bridge is just that—covered, completely covered actually. There's no way anyone could toss anything off the bridge. And the strange noises and splashes might have an easier explanation: it's the sound of the ducks swimming along the Tulpehocken.

This might be a case of "pass on the secret." Like the game where a whispered secret is passed along a line of people, by the time the story gets to the end of the line it usually bears no resemblance to the initial secret.

According to *Ghost Stories of Berks County, Book One*, by Charles J. Adams III, there is a similar story to Penn State Berks haunted bridge. In the late 1800s, Mrs. Bissinger, a mother of three children, was walking with her children along the mule path that follows the Union Canal near Reading. The children were picking up stones and placing them on a basket that was tied around their mother's waist.

At some point, Mrs. Bissinger picked up her children and waded into the deep water. An onlooker ran for help. By the time help arrived, it was too late. Mrs. Bissinger, her children, and her unborn baby drowned.

No one knows why the mother took this fatal action, although some have speculated that she was depressed over the family's financial situation. Others speculate that she was mentally ill.

The story made national headlines and the incident still hasn't completely faded from the area's collective unconscious. In fact, it may not have faded from the area at all. People still claim to see the sad figure of a woman and three children walking along the tow path. It's perhaps a grim reenactment of the gruesome final act.

Adams tells about his own run-in with the spirit powers of the canal. Adams gathered some reporters and took them down the tow path, the same one that the ghosts of Mrs. Bissinger and her children were seen on. Adams had hoped that he and the reporters would see the apparitions. They didn't. However, on the way back from the ghost hunt, a reporter suddenly had trouble breathing. The inexplicable attack lasted for a few seconds; long enough to scare everyone. The reporter said that he had never undergone quite that feeling before, but those familiar with the paranormal would suggest that this was just one way that a troubled spirit—perhaps the troubled spirit of a mother and her murdered children—might reach out to communicate with the living. That's one way to get someone's attention.

People familiar with the canal say the group might not want to jump to conclusions; there are plenty of ghosts to go around. There are reportedly ghosts of Native American tribes and Hessian soldiers that haunt the canal.

Whether these spirits make it to the Berks campus, no one is sure, but it hasn't stopped students from flocking to the campus. According to campus information, in 1972 there were about 500 students; today, nearly 3,000 students attend Penn State Berks.

More than enough to keep the ghost bridge story in circulation.

Penn State Town and Gown Ghosts

Ghost stories of communities near Penn State

The Scotia Ghost

The Scotia Barrens

Its name suggests desolation.

But it wasn't always that way.

At one time, the Scotia Barrens, a swath of mineral-rich land a few miles west of Penn State, was a bit of a boom town in the late 19th, early 20th century Centre County. Iron and steel magnate Andrew Carnegie instantly recognized the value of the minerals discovered there and founded an ironworks on the spot. The site quickly attracted hundreds of workers and small towns like Marysville and Scotia grew up around the ironworks.

But the iron trade didn't last forever and as it faded in Pennsylvania's industrial past, so did the jobs and the towns. The forest reclaimed the area leaving only skeletal remains of factories and homes and, of course, stories about ghosts.

The area is now designated as state game lands for hunters, as well as a hiking trail and sort of a living laboratory for Penn State students, who study the strange anomalies of the Barrens. Hikers and hunters insist it's always a little colder in the Barrens. Then there are the rocks; rusted, red stones that look almost like they're covered with dried blood.

For students who visit the area, it isn't a stretch to believe that a ghost haunts the Barrens.

Folklore suggests they're on to something. Not only does something haunt the Barrens, but people who have had run-ins with it claim that it's a dark force, not the benign spirits that occasionally visit the Penn State campus.

Area folklorists say that the origin of this haunting began during the iron boom. One of the workers who was drawn to the promise of good pay—and no questions—was Bert Delige. Delige had a criminal past. The fact that he was African-American made jobs even scarcer. Perhaps, he looked at a job at the Scotia Ironworks as a new start.

For Delige, it turned not into a new beginning, but a sudden, sad end.

According to newspaper coverage of the case, Delige went on a drunken rampage one night in October, 1910. Police said he spotted the wife of a deceased former boss walking home. He ambushed her and demanded money. He "criminally assaulted" her and then slashed her throat with a razor. The woman died on the trail.

Delige fell under immediate suspicion, but without hard evidence, authorities waited. They didn't need to wait long. Delige took his brother to the place he supposedly stashed the murder weapon. The authorities moved in.

Faced with the overwhelming evidence, Delige confessed.

Delige was convicted for the killing and sentenced to death. According to newspaper reports, Delige was stoic at the gallows. He thanked his jailers and told his brothers to turn from sin. Then, he stepped back onto the trap, the noose limp around his neck.

The trap opened and Delige fell. Besides for a slight twitch of his fingers and a convulsive leg movement, Delige's death seemed painless.

He was buried in a plot near his home

When Delige was hanged in April 25, 1911, it would be the last time a prisoner was hanged in Bellefonte. It also marked the start of the Barrens ghost stories.

There are some at the Barrens who see—or sense—the ghost of a female. Perhaps, it's the murder victim seeking vengeance. Other accounts depict the spirit of a man and there's a feeling of evil or madness.

Since the area is frequented by hunters, more than a few tales are told about the Barrens ghost around hunting camps. According to a story in *The Black Ghost of Scotia & More Fireside Tales*, a group of hunters were using a spotlight to find deer on night. Whether they knew it or not, they ended up in the exact spot where Delige had taken the life of his victim.

The hunters said that they saw a large, shape come to them. It had the profile of a man, but was much larger than an average man. Unlike a ghost, too, it was dark and dense, not like the typical, flimsy spirits you see in movies.

The figure came up on them quickly.

Hunters are generally hard to frighten, but it's easy to imagine this ghostly sight being enough to send even a gnarled backwoodsmen scurrying.

Hunters are also known for their extensive preparations. Apparently, none of the men looked at the calendar—the date of their excursion into the Scotia Barrens was April 25th, the anniversary of Delige's execution.

Since then, while it's never a good time to be trolling around the Barrens alone, people are much more careful to avoid heading into the Barrens on the execution date and the murder date.

The Haunted Granary

Lemont

One Penn State tradition is to spend at least one Halloween visiting the Haunted Lemont Granary festival.

Lemont is a quaint village that hugs the foothills of Mount Nittany. The village, listed on the National Register of Historical Places, is noted for its late Victorian-era homes, historical traditions, and a restored granary. Once a railroad hub for the regions agriculture, the John I Thompson Granary and Coal Sheds was built to help bring the valley's farm produce to market.

The granary underwent an extensive renovation effort in the late 1970s and is now a gleaming reflection of its old glory. While the building has a fresh look, according to legends, it has the same ghosts.

In one legend, the old granary is haunted by an 11-year-old boy. The boy, so the story goes, wandered into the granary with little knowledge of what a dangerous place it could be. Agriculture was—and is—one of the most dangerous occupations. The story states that the boy was in a grain storage area when the grain began to pour out. He was trapped under tons of grain. Eventually, he suffocated and died. Worse yet, months went by before his body was discovered.

Since then, it's said that the ghost haunts the granary and its grounds.

Are there any facts to back up the story? Not really, but that lack of evidence doesn't seem to stop the chattering teeth and occasional shriek of students who visit the granary—all decorated in its spooky finest—on Halloween.

Epilogue

So why are there so many Penn State ghosts?

There are a lot of ghost stories at Penn State, but the jury is still out on whether there are really any ghosts. A deeper question is why is Penn State so haunted, or at least reputed to be so haunted.

As more paranormal investigators have entered the field, the theories about paranormal causes have multiplied. These investigators bring their own backgrounds and perspectives to paranormal causes. These theories are based on everything from folklore to geology to quantum physics. Some could apply to Penn State hauntings.

Eilfie Music, occult specialist for the Penn State Paranormal Research Society, has joined investigations into several haunted spots at Penn State and has heard several theories about the origin of why Penn State is so haunted.

Sacred Ground or Scared Ground?

One theory that has been discussed by paranormal investigators is that the ground underneath the Nittany Valley is sacred, literally.

There is a shelf of limestone and quartz that runs under the valley. Geologically speaking, it's one of the most interesting features in the state.

Access to the limestone made building Penn State facilities, like the original Old Main, much easier. Builders didn't have to truck or carry vast quantities of limestone to the site. They had a ready-made quarry a few yards away from the construction site.

But, some paranormal investigators say the limestone may have made building easier, it made the school more vulnerable to supernatural episodes. The limestone is also highly resonant, almost like crystals that are used in radios and other electronic gear. Some cultures believe that crystals can store magical properties. According to Music, crystals are used in the magical rites of numerous belief systems.

If this is so, advocates of the theory say that Penn State is resting on top of a huge resonating crystal. The psychic energy that emanates from the students and other residents of the valley could be re-emitted at various times and in various forms. Campuses bubble with psychic energy. College students generate a lot of energy. (Residents who are in the downtown area on a Friday night may say they may generate too much energy.)

College campuses are often scenes of tragedies, too. Campuses tend to be small cities and when you have a collection of people—college students or not—there are the normal misfortunes: accidents, suicides, and even murders. These tragic episodes are embedded into the psychic fiber, the experts say.

Paranormal investigators suspect the geological theory is the cause behind residual hauntings on campus. Residual hauntings appear again and again, like spiritual instant replays. Penn State hauntings, like the ghostly actor at Schwab Theater and some manifestations at Pattee Library, could be classified as residual ghosts.

Quantum Possibilities

Ghost busters aren't the only investigators trying to solve the mystery of Penn State hauntings.

While it would be presumptuous to say mainstream physicists have totally embraced the paranormal realm, there are some quantum physicists who are at least embracing the possibility of a paranormal realm and are pitching their own pet theories. Quantum physics looks at the realm of relationships in the very small, and according to Einstein, the very spooky world particles and very discrete units of energy called quanta.

At the quantum level the normal laws of physics melt away, leaving a reality that is based not on hard facts, but on probabilities and possibilities. In this realm, molecules can be at more than one place at a time, particles can pass through solid objects, and things can travel faster than the speed of light. There also seems to be a connection between human consciousness and reality.

In their book, *The Quantum Enigma*, physicists Bruce Rosenblum and Fred Kuttner explore this ghostly world, coming to the conclusion that the theory seems to deny an absolute physical reality independent of consciousness. Most physicists aren't comfortable with this conclusion and have looked for other interpretations for quantum theory.

Over time, quantum physicists have rolled out a parade of theories that explain the *flakiness* of quantum physics. Some of them are almost as weird and almost as scary as visits from dead people and encounters with poltergeists. For instance, there's one theory called the Many Worlds Interpretation that proposes an infinite assortment of universes that contain all possibilities. Instead of the one universe we interact with, there are layers and layers of parallel universes.

This theory is the inspiration of paranormal investigator and writer Paul Eno, who believes there is a connection between parallel worlds and paranormal occurrences. He believes that a connection with the spirit world has nothing to do with death, overactive student imaginations, or even limestone quarries. Ghosts are actually brushes with those parallel universes. Eno speculates that when people see ghosts they are stepping into that filmy region that separates worlds—or universes. In some parallel world, are there ghosts who are frightened or annoyed by encounters with Penn State students?

Psychology 101

Some believe that ghosts on campus have nothing to do with parapsychology and everything to do with psychology. Ghosts, spooks, poltergeists, and urban legends are a natural reaction to college life.

The Penn State freshman, who arrives on the Penn State campus their freshman year, join 40,000 other people from all over the country and all over the globe. Most are away from their family and friends for the very first time. Most have never been subjected to the kinds of academic rigor they'll experience at Penn State. It's a scary new world.

This fear can bubble up in unexpected manners, including ghost stories and legends, according to this theory. "It does make sense that new students on campus have those natural fears and anxieties," Music said. "Telling ghost stories and urban legends is just one way of dealing with those stresses."

Although this theory seems natural, not supernatural, some believers in the paranormal say that this attitude can create real brushes with the paranormal.

If belief is a way for consciousness to translate thought into reality, as some quantum theorists speculate, then tales of ghosts create the right conditions to actually experience ghosts. The task of the paranormal investigator becomes harder to discern real paranormal effects that have origins in the human consciousness from the stories drawn from the human imagination.

Community Building

Another theory, in the folklore vein, is that there's a continual process of community building at Penn State—and other college campuses for that matter. Folklore is a way of building a common story.

It's also one way to build solidarity and make new connections. Stories, such as tales of ghostly campus wanderers and head-lopping ax men, actually unite the students. The students, who come from all different places and backgrounds, suddenly have similar fears and a common history.

Dr. Simon Bronner, a professor at Penn State, Harrisburg and folklore expert, explores this theory in his book, *Piled Higher and Deeper: The Folklore of Campus Life.* Bronner suggests that since a portion of the student population is new to the campus, the urban legends and ghost stories are continually refreshed and create a bond among students.

As the freshmen progress to upper-classmen, they take part in the passing of legends and stories to the newcomers. Those who spent Halloween quivering in their dorm room expecting the next knock on the door to be the campus ax murderer now have a chance to exact a little revenge on newcomers.

Questions

Despite all the solid theories—paranormal and totally normal—mysteries remain.

Just like any college campus, or any place, for that matter, Penn State has been the scene of tragedies and misfortunes.

In 1996 a 19-year-old State College resident took a Mauser rifle to the HUB lawn and began shooting. In the melee that ensued one student was killed and another student was injured. Despite the intense emotions caused by the shooting, the event never spawned an urban legend or a ghost story, at least, not yet.

Similarly, suicides and deadly accidents are rare at Penn State, but not unheard of. It would seem that if the theories are correct on campus folklore every dorm—possibly every floor of every dorm—would have the ghost of some sort. Again, that doesn't seem to be the case.

Even though there are still lots of questions about the hauntings in Penn State—and even questions about whether Penn State is haunted at all—there is still one thing that most students agree on, the legends, ghost stories, and folklore make Penn State an *interesting* place to attend.

Reference

Most of the stories from this book are passed verbally on campus each year, especially during Halloween, but the following books, magazines and newspapers are invaluable resources.

Books

Patty A. Wilson, <u>Pennsylvania Ghost Guide, Vol. 1</u>, Piney Creek Press

Simon J. Bonner, <u>Piled Higher and Deeper: The Folklore of Student Life</u>, August House Publishers

Bruce Rosenblum, Fred Kuttner, <u>Quantum Enigma: Physics Encounters Consciousness</u>, Oxford University Press, USA

Charles J. Adams, II, <u>Ghost Stories of Berks County, Book One</u>, Exeter House Books

Magazines, Newspapers and Blogs

The Penn Stater Magazine

State College Magazine

Town and Gown

The Daily Collegian

The Centre Daily Times

Emily Eppig's Centre Daily Times blog, Centre County Spook (http://community.centredaily.com/?q=blog/1252)

Made in the USA
Middletown, DE
01 February 2024

48952508R00060